THE
EEDS HUDDERSI
MANCHESTER RA

HE STANDEDGE LINE

Martin Bairstow

blished by Martin Bairstow, Fountain Chambers, Halifax, West Yorkshire
inted by Allanwood Press Ltd., Stanningley, Pudsey

Introduction

This is a fully revised and enlarged edition of a title which first appeared in 1984 since when there have been enormous changes on the Trans Pennine route. As before, the text gives a description of the main line between Leeds and Manchester as it appeared in the summer of 1989. This is followed by a historical summary and then a chapter on train services. The various closed branch lines are each dealt with separately.

The first edition included photographs by John Holroyd and Jim Davenport. John worked as a booking clerk at various local stations before taking up a career in which he could utilise his artistic talents more fully. Jim stayed with the railway all his working life. Both of them agreed to let us have the benefit of their reminiscences from the 1950s.

Thanks are due to all the photographers who contributed material both to the original book and for this revised edition. John Holroyd drew the gradient profiles and redrew the maps from my originals. The manuscript was retyped by Jayne Firth.

Halifax, West Yorkshire
January 1990

Martin Bairstow

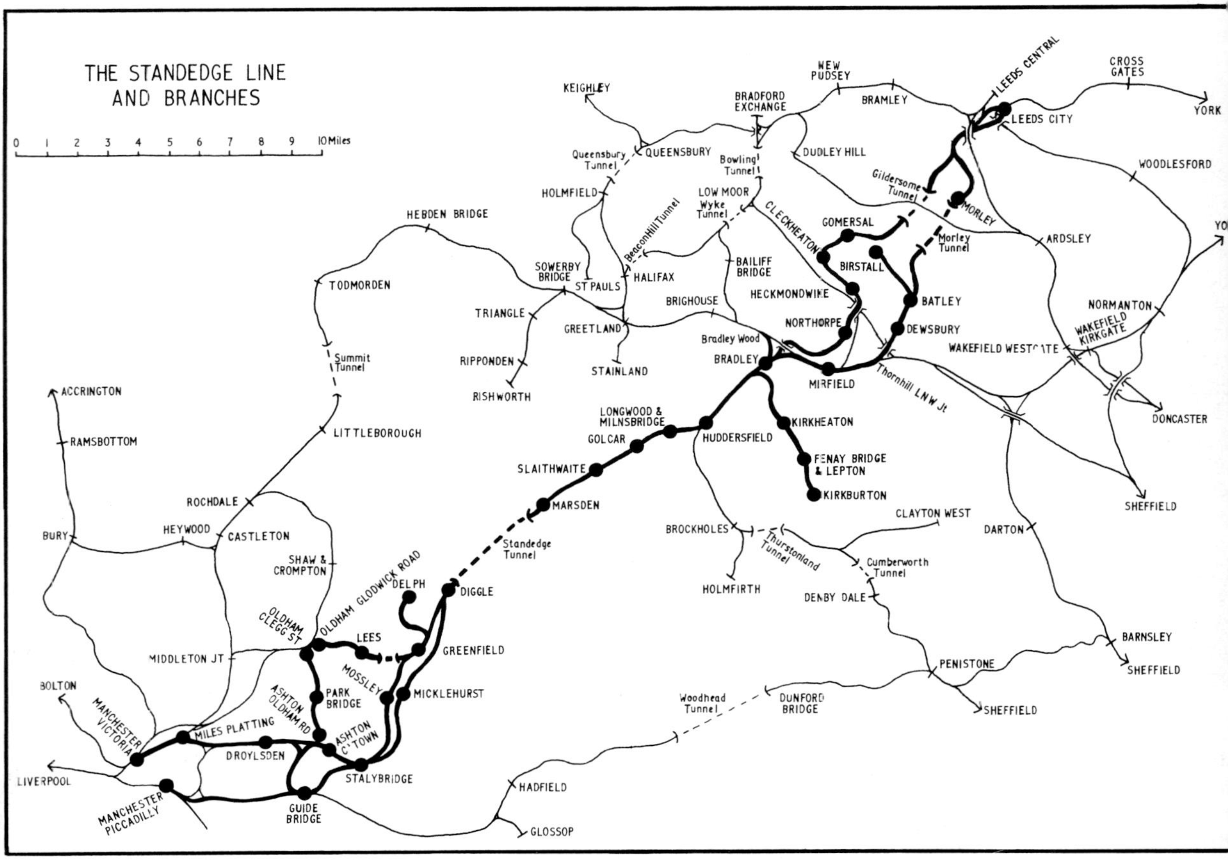

ıemories of Morley Low

y John W. Holroyd

ɟeneral view of Morley Low as it appeared in 1956. *(John Holroyd)*

eturning from a week's holiday in London on aturday 21 April 1956 I discovered that my Station-aster at Stanley had secured a transfer for me to orley Low. Hitherto the winter cycle rides from ildersome to Stanley each day had served to wake e up in the morning but tire me out every evening. orley, on the other hand, was just under two miles om home so now I had a much easier journey and ould travel home for lunch.

I reported for duty on St Georges Day, Monday 3 April at 08.30 and the former clerk briefly showed e the ropes before heading to his new posting. tationmaster Miles had moved from Morley to irkstall some weeks earlier so for another few weeks e were to be in the hands of relief stationmasters. orters Wilf Horner and Dennis Wilby alternated early nd late turns on a weekly basis whilst, as clerk, I ccupied the 'middle' turn with Wednesday and aturday afternoons free alternately with the Station-aster or his relief.

The Booking Office formed the upper floor of the tationmaster's Office with the ticket window looking ut to a lobby at the head of stairs for the Leeds-ound platform. There was a door to the street and e other exit from this lobby led directly onto the otbridge and the up platform. First job on day two was to number all the cupboards and drawers in my cosy, gas lit, coal heated room and to make a 'Where is it' book. Passing trains were easily seen from this vantage point once the daily tasks of book-balancing and coal waybilling had been accomplished. Most small stations in the area received coal waybills from a colliery – Morley Low looking after South Kirkby – and individual bills, carbon copies and Hollerith cards were to be made out and despatched in a canvas bag to the Revenue Accountant at Peterborough. For charging purposes the Swinton & Knottingley or the West Riding & Grimsby routes taken by South Kirkby coal had to be differentiated. The record daily batch of waybills I documented was 199. This amounted to a total of 2216 tons 14 cwt. Only respite from this task was the colliery's annual holiday at the end of July.

Each day's takings were sent in a wax-sealed leather bag accompanied by signed papers exchanged with the guard of its transporting train to Leeds. On Fridays the Stationmaster and I would walk up to the Bank in town and collect money for the wages. The Stationmaster normally worked out the payslips and put the cash into envelopes. Besides the immediate staff at Morley Low which included the signalmen and gangers, the part-time box at Ward's Siding (now the site of Cottingley Station) and the signalmen and gangers at Gildersome East on the 'New Line' also came on Morley's payroll. For this reason the Stationmaster's house was situated on Rooms Lane, about mid-way between Morley Low and Gildersome East—but not very handy for any trains! One Friday the signalwoman from Ward's Siding and one of Morley's signalmen decided to elope, but not before they'd met the Stationmaster and me in town to collect their pay packets.

One of the surprises of clerical life was the way in which one or two auditors would arrive out of the blue, usually about once a year, and pore over the books, tickets, parcel labels and check that the kettle was working. Each month it was incumbent on the clerk to make out something like twenty assorted forms relating to financial and statistical matters. Our one season ticket holder who travelled almost daily to Stalybridge retired; for the next 12 months the 'Pink Return' had to contain an explanation of this change in takings from the previous years' equivalent week!

Duty called on Sunday 20 May to book six excursion trains and on Whit Monday another train to Blackpool was so full on leaving Leeds that some refunds had to be given to would-be-trippers. The weekend produced takings of £417. Monday 28 May saw the installation of Dennis Cross as permane Stationmaster, his move being from Headingley. N pay packet with the past weekend's overtime came £4.10s.4d. Ackroyd Street Working Mens Club r two trainloads to the Lancashire coast on Saturd 2 June and local Sunday Schools combined also to a special train. On 23 June an excursion from Lee hauled by 4F 44019 came to a halt in the tunnel wi injector trouble. It reversed into the sidings and tv hours later 8F 48188 came from Farnley shed to ta the rather cheerless trippers on their way. Driv Haley, a near neighbour of ours in Gildersom suffered the derailment of his WD 90620 on the poin into the down sidings on Friday 26 April 1957. It w hauled back onto the tracks two hours later.

The crossover in front of the signal box saw fai frequent use because of the carriage storage sidin adjacent to the up, southbound line. Twice the wi operating the 'dolly' signal for this crossover came c its pulley within the confines of the signal-box fran causing delay to services. Occasionally porters Denr or Wilf would help me to affix seat reservation ticke and coach numbers to the stock parked in the sidings. The carriages also served as a useful source soap for our office washbasin.

A Manchester to Leeds stopper picks up Saturday shoppers at Morley Low on 13 April 1957. *(John Holroyd)*

Another infrequent activity was to carry baskets of
geons out onto the nearby hillocks and release em, noting the time on the label, then sending the sket on its way home too. Parcels could be brought Morley Low for despatch by rail but deliveries and llections in the Morley area were handled by one of e vans based at Batley station. The only regular ms labelled 'To be called for'. I once took two dgies to a house in Fountain Street rather than bmit them to the additional van ride.

Cleaners arrived to give the whole station a orough scrubbing in early August 1956 and three inters came on 11 February 1957 to decorate the emises. I recall accompanying the painters on a half our trip into the tunnel on a ballast train but it was a nokey experience.

So the routine continued until Monday 15 April 1957 when trainee clerk Ada Smith arrived for instruction in booking office practise. This was a busy time for passengers with many weekend excursions. I worked from 0800 until 1200 on Sunday 21 April taking £94.4s.0½d and the following day produced £192.0s.0d. This compares with the entire December 1956 month-end of £171.9s.3d. We were advised that once Ada was competent I would be transferred to Leeds City so my last full day at Morley Low was Saturday 8 June 1957. I continued to use the station to park my bike and travel to Leeds on the train although it was actually quicker to cycle direct from Gildersome to Leeds, but a more hilly return in the evening.

The sums of money quoted in this article should be multiplied by a factor of 12 to arrive at their equivalent 1990 value.

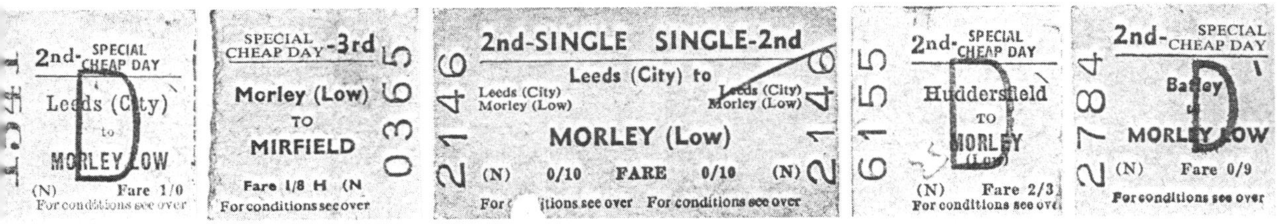

MEMENTOS OF MORLEY LOW

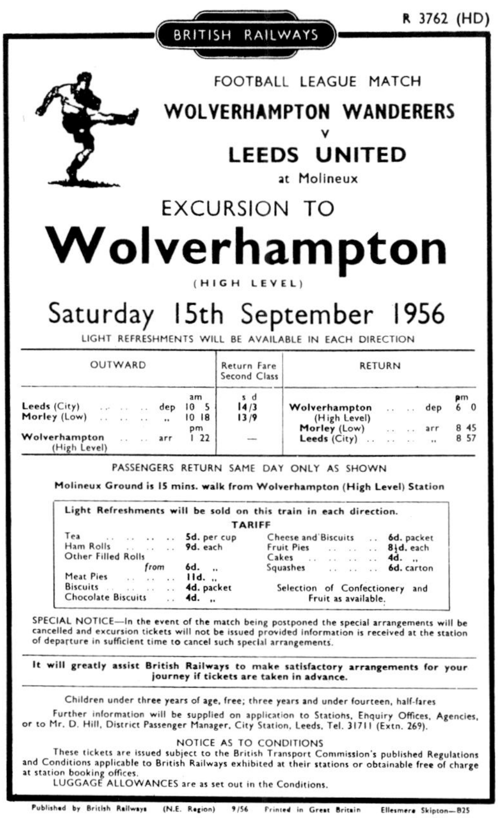

R 3762 (HD)

BRITISH RAILWAYS

FOOTBALL LEAGUE MATCH

WOLVERHAMPTON WANDERERS
v
LEEDS UNITED
at Molineux

EXCURSION TO

Wolverhampton

(HIGH LEVEL)

Saturday 15th September 1956

LIGHT REFRESHMENTS WILL BE AVAILABLE IN EACH DIRECTION

OUTWARD			Return Fare Second Class	RETURN		
		am	s d			pm
Leeds (City)	dep	10 5	14/3	**Wolverhampton** (High Level)	dep	6 0
Morley (Low)	,,	10 18	13/9	**Morley** (Low)	arr	8 45
		pm		**Leeds** (City)	,,	8 57
Wolverhampton (High Level)	arr	1 22	—			

PASSENGERS RETURN SAME DAY ONLY AS SHOWN

Molineux Ground is 15 mins. walk from Wolverhampton (High Level) Station

Light Refreshments will be sold on this train in each direction.

TARIFF

Tea	**5d.** per cup	Cheese and Biscuits	**6d.** packet
Ham Rolls	**9d.** each	Fruit Pies	**8½d.** each
Other Filled Rolls *from*	**6d.** ,,	Cakes	**4d.** ,,
Meat Pies	**11d.** ,,	Squashes	**6d.** carton
Biscuits	**4d.** packet	Selection of Confectionery and Fruit as available.	
Chocolate Biscuits	**4d.** ,,		

SPECIAL NOTICE—In the event of the match being postponed the special arrangements will be cancelled and excursion tickets will not be issued provided information is received at the station of departure in sufficient time to cancel such special arrangements.

It will greatly assist British Railways to make satisfactory arrangements for your journey if tickets are taken in advance.

Children under three years of age, free; three years and under fourteen, half-fares

Further information will be supplied on application to Stations, Enquiry Offices, Agencies, or to Mr. D. Hill, District Passenger Manager, City Station, Leeds, Tel. 31711 (Extn. 269).

NOTICE AS TO CONDITIONS

These tickets are issued subject to the British Transport Commission's published Regulations and Conditions applicable to British Railways exhibited at their stations or obtainable free of charge at station booking offices.

LUGGAGE ALLOWANCES are as set out in the Conditions.

Published by British Railways (N.E. Region) 9/56 Printed in Great Britain Ellesmere Skipton—B25

R 2198 (HD)

BRITISH RAILWAYS

DIESEL EXCURSION

TO

BLACKPOOL

(CENTRAL)

Sunday 22nd May 1960

OUTWARD			Return Fares Second Class	RETURN		
		a.m.	s d			p.m.
Leeds (City)	dep.	10 5	11/6	**Blackpool** (Central)	dep.	6 50
Morley (Low)	,,	10 15	11/6	**Marsden**	arr.	8 45
Batley	,,	10 25	11/0	**Slaithwaite**	,,	8 50
Dewsbury (W. Rd.)	,,	10 29	10/6	**Huddersfield**	,,	9 2
Mirfield	,,	10 36	10/6	**Mirfield**	,,	9 14
Huddersfield	,,	10 47	10/6	**Dewsbury** (W. Rd.)	,,	9 23
Slaithwaite	,,	11 0	10/6	**Batley**	,,	9 29
Marsden	,,	11 8	10/0	**Morley** (Low)	,,	9 39
		p.m.		**Leeds** (City)	,,	9 51
Blackpool (Central)	arr.	1 2	—			

PASSENGERS RETURN SAME DAY ONLY AS SHOWN

Children under three years of age, free; three years and under fourteen, half-fares
(Fractions of 1d. reckoned as 1d.)

Tickets can be obtained IN ADVANCE at the stations or accredited rail ticket Agencies

Further information will be supplied on application to Stations, Enquiry Offices, Agencies, or to Mr. D. Hill, District Passenger Superintendent, City Station, Leeds, Tel. 31711, Extn. 269, (Office hours 9—5 Mon. to Fri. 9—12 Sat.).

NOTICE AS TO CONDITIONS

These tickets are issued subject to the Regulations and Conditions in the Commission's Publications and Notices applicable to British Railways. Luggage Allowances are as set out in the Conditions.

Published by British Railways (N.E. Region) 4/60 Printed in Great Britain Ellesmere, Skipton—C4

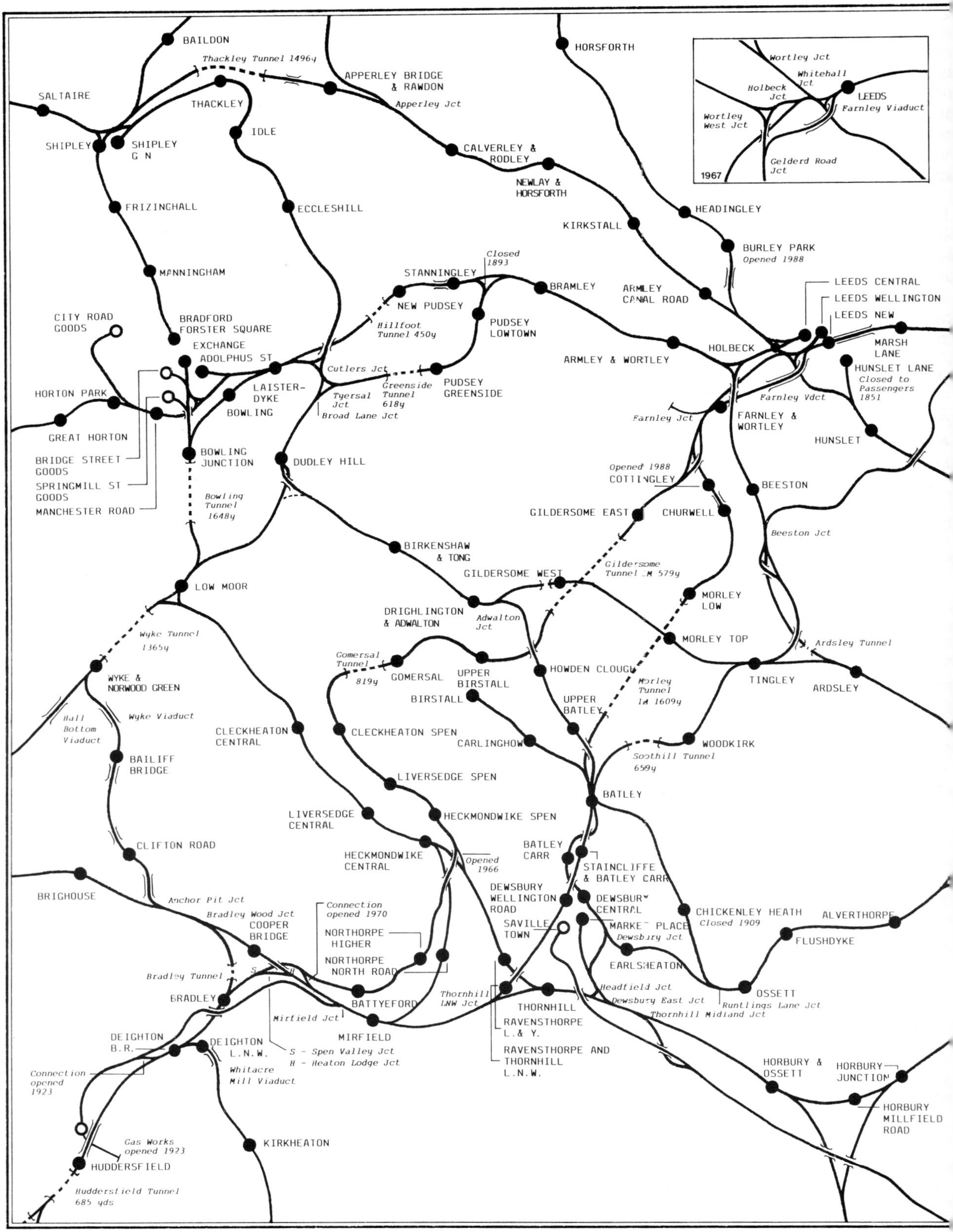

BAILDON
Thackley Tunnel 1496y
SALTAIRE
THACKLEY
APPERLEY BRIDGE & RAWDON
Apperley Jct
HORSFORTH
SHIPLEY
SHIPLEY G N
IDLE
CALVERLEY & RODLEY
NEWLAY & HORSFORTH
FRIZINGHALL
ECCLESHILL
HEADINGLEY
KIRKSTALL
BURLEY PARK
Opened 1988
MANNINGHAM
Closed 1893
STANNINGLEY
BRAMLEY
ARMLEY CANAL ROAD
LEEDS CENTRAL
LEEDS WELLINGTON
LEEDS NEW
NEW PUDSEY
CITY ROAD GOODS
BRADFORD FORSTER SQUARE
PUDSEY LOWTOWN
Hillfoot Tunnel 450y
MARSH LANE
EXCHANGE
ADOLPHUS ST
HOLBECK
ARMLEY & WORTLEY
HUNSLET LANE
Closed to Passengers 1851
Cutlers Jct
LAISTER-DYKE
PUDSEY GREENSIDE
Greenside Tunnel 618y
HORTON PARK
Tyersal Jct
Broad Lane Jct
BOWLING
Farnley Vdct
Farnley Jct
FARNLEY & WORTLEY
GREAT HORTON
HUNSLET
BRIDGE STREET GOODS
BOWLING JUNCTION
DUDLEY HILL
SPRINGMILL ST GOODS
Opened 1988
COTTINGLEY
BEESTON
MANCHESTER ROAD
Bowling Tunnel 1648y
GILDERSOME EAST
CHURWELL
Beeston Jct
BIRKENSHAW & TONG
GILDERSOME WEST
Gildersome Tunnel 579y
LOW MOOR
MORLEY LOW
DRIGHLINGTON & ADWALTON
Adwalton Jct
MORLEY TOP
Ardsley Tunnel
Wyke Tunnel 1365y
Gomersal Tunnel 819y
GOMERSAL
UPPER BIRSTALL
HOWDEN CLOUGH
TINGLEY
ARDSLEY
WYKE & NORWOOD GREEN
BIRSTALL
Morley Tunnel 1609y
Hall Bottom Viaduct
Wyke Viaduct
UPPER BATLEY
CLECKHEATON CENTRAL
CLECKHEATON SPEN
CARLINGHOW
WOODKIRK
BAILIFF BRIDGE
Soothill Tunnel 659y
LIVERSEDGE SPEN
BATLEY
LIVERSEDGE CENTRAL
HECKMONDWIKE SPEN
CLIFTON ROAD
HECKMONDWIKE CENTRAL
BATLEY CARR
Opened 1966
STAINCLIFFE & BATLEY CARR
BRIGHOUSE
Anchor Pit Jct
DEWSBURY WELLINGTON ROAD
DEWSBURY CENTRAL
CHICKENLEY HEATH
Closed 1909
ALVERTHORPE
Connection opened 1970
Bradley Wood Jct
COOPER BRIDGE
SAVILLE TOWN
MARKET PLACE
Dewsbury Jct
FLUSHDYKE
NORTHORPE HIGHER
NORTHORPE NORTH ROAD
EARLSHEATON
Bradley Tunnel
S
H
Headfield Jct
OSSETT
Thornhill LNW Jct
Dewsbury East Jct
Runtlings Lane Jct
BRADLEY
BATTYEFORD
THORNHILL
Thornhill Midland Jct
Mirfield Jct
RAVENSTHORPE L. & Y.
MIRFIELD
DEIGHTON B.R.
DEIGHTON L.N.W.
S - Spen Valley Jct
H - Heaton Lodge Jct
RAVENSTHORPE AND THORNHILL L.N.W.
HORBURY & OSSETT
HORBURY JUNCTION
Connection opened 1923
Whitacre Mill Viaduct
HORBURY MILLFIELD ROAD
Gas Works opened 1923
KIRKHEATON
HUDDERSFIELD
Huddersfield Tunnel 685 yds
Wortley Jct
Whitehall Jct
Holbeck Jct
LEEDS
Farnley Viaduct
Wortley West Jct
Gelderd Road Jct
1967

A Trans-Pennine Journey

Leeds enjoys the advantage of having all its railway services concentrated in one centrally situated station. When the present arrangements were planned in the 1960s, it was envisaged that there would be little more than a third the number of trains now using the station which handles up to 30 arrivals and 30 departures per hour at peak times.

The present station was opened in 1869 jointly by the London & North Western and the North Eastern Railways. It carried the name Leeds New until 1938 when it was amalgamated with the older adjacent Wellington Station to become Leeds City. As part of the scheme to permit closure of the nearby Leeds Central in 1967, Leeds New was rebuilt and enlarged to accommodate all passenger trains whilst the former Wellington platforms became the exclusive preserve of parcels traffic.

The passenger station has 12 platforms, five through of which three are electrified, five bays at the west end and two at the east. 'Trans-Pennine' expresses for Manchester usually depart from platform 12 which was built in 1961 on the outside of the original train shed. In the opposite direction platform 9 on the other non electrified through line is normally used by trains bound for Hull, Scarborough and Newcastle.

If the train is from Newcastle to Liverpool, it will comprise a class 47 loco hauling about six non air conditioned mark 2 coaches in a special 'Trans-Pennine' livery of blue and white. Trains from Hull and Scarborough are generally worked by class 156 'super sprinters' often in formation of only two coaches. Although these trains seat more passengers per coach than did older rolling stock, they can be very crowded especially between Leeds, Dewsbury and Huddersfield where the West Yorkshire PTE has ordained that cheap fares should be charged. Outside the Monday to Friday peak period it is even free to senior citizens.

The River Aire flows under the station itself. The Leeds & Liverpool Canal passes under the railway just outside at what used to be called Canal Junction but which BR renamed Leeds City East Junction. The route which diverges here on to a long viaduct was built in 1882 to provide Huddersfield trains with a non conflicting exit from Leeds to Farnley Junction. Unfortunately in the 1960s the viaduct line was disconnected from the Huddersfield route and commandeered for use by trains to London via a new junction at Gelderd Road. In 1987, as part of the electrification works, London trains were put back onto their older Holbeck route leaving Farnley Viaduct as just a head shunt for trains switching platforms in Leeds Station.

All of which is unfortunate because the viaduct line would have taken Huddersfield traffic straight out of platforms 9 and 12 avoiding three busy junctions at Leeds City West, Whitehall and Holbeck. However, plans now exist to remodel the western approaches to Leeds Station providing six rather than four tracks at the critical point and once more giving an independent exit for Huddersfield trains running parallel with the present route. Until this happens, the layout will continue to be severely congested.

At Leeds City West Junction, we part company with what was the Midland Main Line to Sheffield, Birmingham and London but which now carries a half hourly local train to Castleford. For the short distance to Whitehall Junction, we are on the former Midland Railway whose line continues through the Aire Valley towards Skipton. We ascend a steep curve, built in 1967, to reach the level of the GNR route coming out of Leeds Central. Having so climbed, the Huddersfield line immediately leaves those to Bradford and Wakefield at Holbeck East Junction and drops back down

A Trans-Pennine unit pulls out of Leeds Station on a Hull to Liverpool Lime Street working in April 1961. *(P. Sunderland)*

Hughes Fowler 'crab' 2-6-0 No. 42721 and 'Jubilee' 4-6-0 No. 45666 'Cornwallis' await departure from Leeds City with an express for Manchester Exchange via the Standedge route on 23 July 1955. *(B.K.B. Green)*

to its old level. A siding marks the course of the pre 1967 LNWR curve from Whitehall Junction. Under the new plans that alignment will come back into use to give Huddersfield trains a faster non conflicting exit from Leeds.

We go under the Wakefield line which uses a short viaduct to span not just the two running lines but also the space occupied by sidings which made up the LNWR goods yard at this point. The remains of a station building can be detected at Farnley & Wortley. This is the pre 1882 establishment. From that year until 1952, there was a station nearby on the viaduct route out of Leeds.

Farnley Junction was the meeting point of the two routes out of Leeds and the divergence of the 'old' and 'new' lines to Huddersfield. The engine shed, which was opened in 1885 to replace an earlier LNWR shed nearer to Leeds, stood in the angle formed by the Farnley goods branch. That branch is still in use serving a steel stockyard and is the only visible reminder that there ever was such a place as Farnley Junction. The signal box here closed in December 1966 when the viaduct route was taken out of use.

The 'Leeds New Line' to Huddersfield via the Spen Valley was built on a grand scale and left the older route by a flying junction. One can still make out the single track bed of the down (Leeds bound) line climbing away to the right and the parapets of the up line bridge which used to go across the Dewsbury route.

Cottingley Station was opened by the PTE in 19ε
to serve a substantial housing estate. An earli
station at Churwell stood a little further south beyor
the seven arch viaduct with platforms approached b
separate staircases up from the road. Then the railwa
makes a long sweep towards Morley, where the Tow
Hall stands prominently on the skyline. The town use
to be better served by the appropriately named Morle
Top Station on the Great Northern Railway. The e
LNW station at Morley Low is about a mile from th
town centre but this is the nearest that the trains ca
get because just beyond the end of the platforms th
line plunges into the 1 mile 1,609 yards long tunnel

Emerging from Morley Tunnel, the line soon passe
between the supports of the bridge which carried th
GNR Bradford to Wakefield line. Hiding behind th
abutment on the right hand side is Lady Anne Cros
ing signal box which is now called Batley and is th
only manual box, albeit with all colour light signal
between the areas covered by Leeds and Healey Mil
power boxes.

As the GN and LNW routes come together on th
approach to Batley they were joined on their respe
tive sides of the layout by their branches from Beesto
and from Birstall. Batley Station had five throug
platforms serving the two railways plus a bay for th
Birstall branch and an isolated platform at an angle bu
linked by a footbridge to cater for the Chickenle
Heath line. Now just two platforms survive for th
Leeds – Huddersfield trains. All the other lines hav

ɜen closed and the rest of the station area has been developed. Batley was one of the last 'local' stations West Yorkshire to remain staffed but the booking fice closed on 2 September 1989.

We leave Batley by a viaduct alongside which the rmer Great Northern formation drops down to the ft then passes under the LNW route twice before aching Dewsbury. Here the LNW, L&Y and GN ailways managed to provide three separate unconected stations and the Midland nearly produced a urth. The LNWR station at Wellington Road is the ıly survivor. We enter it by a viaduct. To the left is a m of shoddy and mungo manufacturers still trading om a five storey stone mill blackened by generations railway, industrial and domestic soot.

Shortly after we have left Dewsbury, the River alder comes close to the railway on the left hand de. At the other side of the river is Savile Town to hich the Midland Railway opened its rather ill fated anch at the beginning of this century. We cross the alder by a viaduct and have a view to the right of the nger but lower structure carrying the disused ornhill to Heckmondwike branch which goes under ır line. We next cross the canal and then enter avensthorpe Station. This has for many years esented a tumbledown appearance. The derelict te of what was Thornhill power station on the right as yet to be redeveloped.

Immediately beyond Ravensthorpe platforms is ornhill LNW Junction where the original Leeds & Dewsbury Railway ends. For the next 2½ miles, the Leeds – Huddersfield – Manchester route shares the tracks of its older rival, the Calder Valley Line. Historically this section was a bottleneck and had to be quadrupled over 100 years ago but since realignment of the junctions in 1988, three tracks have sufficed. The River Calder is crossed before we reach the site of Cleckheaton Junction which brought in the ex L&Y branch from Bradford via the Spen Valley, closed in 1965. Mirfield Station was a wide island platform with overall roof and bays at the east end. The remains have recently been tidied up to provide the most basic facilities for passengers at what is now a bare, windswept, unstaffed platform.

Just beyond Mirfield, the Calder is recrossed at a rather wide point adjacent to a weir. Opposite the remains of Mirfield (L&Y) motive power depot is the site of the junction which marked the start of the Midland Railway's futile branch into Huddersfield.

Before we part company with the Calder Valley route at Heaton Lodge, there can be seen on the right, the partial remains of Battyeford Viaduct which used to bring the Leeds New Line to a point alongside Heaton Lodge Junction. Trains for Huddersfield and Manchester simply branch off to the left but those in the opposite direction burrow under the Calder Valley line using the 'New Line' formation. The point where the 'up' and 'down' lines now rejoin south of Heaton Lodge used to be Spen Valley Junction.

The route from Heaton Lodge as far as Marsden has

A class 40 stands with a Newcastle to Liverpool express in June 1961 at platform 17 (now No. 12) which had been opened the previous week. A named 'black five' occupies the adjacent track. *(P. Sunderland)*

been reduced from quadruple to double track except in the immediate vicinity of Huddersfield Station. Investment in higher speeds has involved the slewing of the running lines from one side of the track bed to the other. The single track which curves in at Bradley is disused, the regular service from Halifax having ceased in 1965. Nothing remains of the four platform Bradley Station which closed in 1950 but a mile further on we come upon the wooden halt at Deighton built in 1982. An earlier Deighton Station, closed in 1930, was a few yards down the Kirkburton branch which joined at this point.

The abandoned railway formation which descends on our right to come level at Red Doles is the Midland Huddersfield branch. An expanse of railway owned land on the right at Hillhouse is now derelict but was once the site of the LNWR engine shed and both the LNW and L&Y goods depots.

The final approach to Huddersfield is by a long viaduct which used to carry five tracks. From the inside, the station appears unspectacular. It is only by stepping outside that one can appreciate the length to which the LNW and L&Y Railways went to provide a structure worthy of the accord which had enabled them jointly to bring the benefits of railway communication to this town. The central building which was once a hotel has a projecting portico supported by eight 68 feet high Corinthian columns. On either side a colonade leads to smaller buildings at the two ends of the 416 feet long frontage. These are also fronted by four columns and at one time housed the separate LNW and L&Y booking offices. Nowadays the travel centre is in the main building.

The station had eight platforms but only five remain in use. Leeds to Manchester trains call at platform 1 which adjoins the main building. The subway leads an island platform, the outer face of which (No. 8) used by Trans-Pennine services in the opposite dire tion. The inner face (No. 4) is generally used by trai to and from Sheffield whilst 2 bays (Nos. 5 & 6) at t north end are available for local trains starting f Leeds and Wakefield.

The platforms lead directly into the twin Hudder field Tunnels. The line comes briefly into the open Springwood Junction where the Sheffield trai branch off then immediately enters Gledholt Tunn also a twin bore now with one track in each.

Behind to the left, there is a good view of Paddo Viaduct on the Sheffield line as the train climbs aw up the Colne Valley. A rock cutting leads to the site Longwood & Milnsbridge Station. Then the line carried over the 20 arch Milnsbridge Viaduct befo passing the once extensive Longwood goods yar Golcar Station has disappeared but Slaithwaite can back to life in 1982 as a PTE halt with stagger platforms. It is located between two large viaducts

The Colne Valley, below on the left, still hous some textile mills who were encouraged to move u the valley when the opening of the railway made co more readily available. The scenery becomes mo rural as we draw towards Marsden which retains manual box controlling a mixture of semaphore ar colour light signals. When the route was 'dequa rified' a loop was retained so that freight travelli towards Manchester could take refuge and be ove taken by passenger trains. With the increas frequency since sprinterisation, most freight has h to be rerouted via the Calder Valley and the proble became one of finding somewhere for the stoppi trains to seek refuge from the expresses. In 1989,

A 'Jinty' 0-6-0 tank descends the Whitehall curve in July 1961 with a transfer freight for Neville Hill. Holbeck High Level Station is on the embankment. *(P. Sunderland)*

Class 40 No. D274 negotiates the curves of Farnley Viaduct as it takes the 1882 exit from Leeds and crosses over the ex-Midland line alongside Holbeck Shed. The train is the 9.45 am Newcastle to Liverpool Lime Street on 10 March 1961. *(G.W. Morrison)*

›w platform was provided on the loop for trains rminating at Marsden.

Standedge Tunnel is the third longest on British ailways. To the left of the present double line tunnel e the two single line bores which were taken out of e in 1966. The canal tunnel starts by the restored ilding on the right of the railway which is now a urist information centre. It immediately passes der the line to occupy a position between the uble and single railway bores but at a lower level.

Diggle is rather a remote spot. Its station, closed in 68, has all but disappeared but Diggle Junction box mains as a block post and to control the goods loop the down (Leeds) side. It is no longer called upon to gnal trains onto the Micklehurst Loop – the duplite line which ran down the east side of the Tame alley as far as Stalybridge. The ruins of Saddleworth ation lead immediately onto the viaduct beyond hich the short Delph branch used to trail in on the ght. It is possible to make out the foundation of elph Junction box and the waiting room at oorgate Halt which was only served by trains to and om Delph.

Greenfield is still open though with a less frequent rvice than stations on the Yorkshire side. The bay atform leading the first few yards along the Oldham e is derelict and the name of the signal box, reenfield Junction, is 25 years out of date. Mossley ation occupies a narrow dark spot in a cutting. One n appreciate the difficulty which would have been ncountered if the LNWR had attempted to quadruple this section of line.

Brick built cotton mills have taken the place of the stone built woollen manufactories on the other side of the Pennines but nowhere do they dominate the landscape to anything like the extent which they used to. A tunnel leads into Stalybridge. The Micklehurst Loop used to have its own parallel tunnel. The station is rather exposed without its platform canopies. Stalybridge used to serve as the frontier between three companies. The main station was the joint property of the LNW and Great Central Railways. The L&Y had a separate but adjacent station on the north side. Since May 1989 the hourly trains from Scarborough or Newcastle to Liverpool have continued to Manchester Piccadilly along the ex Great Central route via Guide Bridge. A connection to Manchester Victoria is provided by the hourly North Wales train which arrives in the down (Leeds bound) platform discharges its passengers and then sets back to cross over and await its return departure from the bay at the Manchester end of the up platform. The hourly Hull to Manchester Piccadilly trains do not stop at Stalybridge.

After parting company with the line to Victoria, the ex GC route drops at 1 in 138 for ¾ mile then skirts the town of Ashton Under Lyne. There used to be a station at Park Parade just before the nine arch viaduct which carries the line over the River Tame. On the east side of the line, there are odd remains of the LNWR branch from Stalybridge to Denton Junction which used to run closely parallel to the Great Central.

There was also a station at Dukinfield, south of Ashton Viaduct just before the bridge by which the railway recrosses the Tame. From this point there are gantries spanning the line which used to support the overhead wires installed for the benefit of transfer freight when the Woodhead line was electrically operated. The approach to Guide Bridge is marked by a mass of derelict sidings a few of which are still used to store the odd diesel locomotive. At the entrance to Guide Bridge Station we join the electrified route from Glossop and Hadfield – the rump of what was the main line from Sheffield via Woodhead Tunnel. All traffic has been concentrated since 1984 on the two platforms on the north side of the station.

There remain a handful of trains which run from Stalybridge to Stockport. These branch off to the left immediately after leaving Guide Bridge. Prior to May 1989 the service was hourly and provided a valuable link for long distance travellers but they can now connect at Piccadilly. On our right there used to be a triangular junction with the Oldham, Ashton & Guide Bridge Junction line which is featured later in the book. All this is now lifted but we pass under a railway bridge carrying the line between Denton and Ashton Moss North Junctions now used largely for freight.

The route from Guide Bridge to Ashburys used to be quadruple. The present double track keeps to the south side of the formation but it is possible that rails may eventually be relaid on the other side if the Glossop and Hadfield line becomes part of the Manchester Metro.

Fairfield Station was on the junction with t abandoned branch to Fallowfield. It had six platfor but now finds itself semi derelict and somewh remote. The PTE has looked into the possibility moving it eastward nearer to Audenshaw. The ot spur from the Fallowfield line still curves in sharply j before Gorton Station. The next stretch of line pass through what was a major centre of locomotive bui ing with the Great Central Gorton Works on the no side of the line and Beyer Peacock directly opposi

Local trains from New Mills use the former Gr Central and Midland Joint line which joins our route the entrance to Ashburys Station. The New Mills s vice is also proposed for incorporation into t Manchester Metro. The route from Ashburys Ardwick passes what was a mass of sidings. Th used to be a triangular junction with the L&Y bran to Miles Platting. The curve from Ashburys is still use but a partly demolished brick viaduct marks t route taken by the curve to Ardwick. The station he which is served only by trains from the New Mills li is reached just before we come alongside the fo track main line from Stockport. There are then lines for the remainder of the journey in Manchester. If our train is terminating it will run in the main part of Piccadilly Station where there are platforms. The station used to be shared by the Gr Central which occupied platforms 1 to 3 and t LNWR which had the rest. It was substantia modernised in the early 1960s in anticipation of elec fication of the service to London. A further facelift h

A Liverpool to Newcastle express passing Farnley & Wortley Station which had closed in 1952, though it was still used by railway staff working at Farnley Junction Shed. *(P. Sunderland)*

:ently taken place to mark the transfer of Trans-nnine and other trains to Piccadilly. The biggest ange has been the doubling in length of the island tform (nos 13 and 14) which is situated at an angle the main station. It is this 'appendix' to Manchester :cadilly which is used by trains travelling through to erpool as well as to Altrincham, Blackpool and uthport. It is very congested though some relief is omised when the Altrincham service is diverted to the metro.

alybridge to Manchester Victoria

ains for Manchester Victoria leave the Piccadilly ıte at Stalybridge by a 15 mph curve. A succession overbridge leads to the island platform at Ashton arlestown. This is the sole survivor of a number of tions which once served the town of Ashton Under ne. Despite its proximity to the town centre it has ıg suffered an infrequent local service with long ps outside of the peak periods.

Passengers noticing the name of the next signal box ll require some knowledge of railway history to ow what is meant by OA & GB Junction. This is ıere the LNWR/Great Central Joint Line from dham Clegg Street joined the L&Y then imme-ıtely diverged at the other side in the direction of ıide Bridge. The Oldham line was removed some ıe ago and the junction will disappear completely if e little used curve to Ashton Moss is finally closed. ith it will go a feature which was once very familiar junction signals with the distants for the next box neath the homes.

The third leg of the triangle trails in at Ashton Moss Junction and is still fairly well used. A more direct route from Stockport used to curve in at Droylsden Station which is closed and demolished. Between here and the next closed station at Clayton Bridge the line crosses the Medlock Valley on a ten arch viaduct. Park Station is served by a few rush hour trains. A goods branch joins at Philips Park No. 1 box and leaves again on the other side at Ashton Branch Sidings to reach Brewery Sidings where it joins the line to Rochdale.

Only a handful of trains call at the sharply curved platforms at Miles Platting though the station is well served by trains on the Rochdale and Oldham lines. In the 1984 edition of this book, Miles Platting was described as quite well maintained but since then the buildings have been demolished leaving just a spartan unstaffed halt.

The final descent into Manchester is down the 1 in 47 bank which had to be rope worked for a short time after its opening in 1844 but that was before completion of the Standedge Line.

The electrified line from Bury passes under our line by a tunnel, then draws level on the left hand side to reach one of the suburban platforms at Victoria. Traditionally L&Y local trains from Stalybridge would also go into the suburban station but the LNWR expresses would pass through the main line part of Victoria to reach their own Exchange Station. Happily for the travelling public this latter facility was closed in 1969 and the Stalybridge to North Wales train now calls at platform 11. This was claimed to be the longest platform in Europe when, with a total length of 2,238 feet, it also served as platform 3 in Exchange Station.

The afternoon Heaton to Manchester (Red Bank) empty newspaper vans passing Wards Siding, now the site of Cottingley Station, on 16 August 1962 behind 45232 and 45737 'Atlas'. The rear of the train is passing under the 'New Line' flyover. *(M. Mitchell)*

46145 'The Duke of Wellington's Regiment (West Riding)' gathers rust outside Farnley Junction shed on 10 August 1963. *(Martin Bairstow collection)*

'Jubilee' class 4-6-0 No. 45463 'Rodney' passing Cottingley with a Saturdays only Blackpool – Leeds on 8 August 1964. The prefabs have since made way for a more modern housing estate. *(M. Mitchell)*

A class 156 'Super Sprinter' crossing Churwell Viaduct on a Hull to Manchester trip. Amongst the defects of these vehicles is the inability of the seat bottoms to remain fixed to their fixtures, making it difficult to find a firm position for one's own bottom! *(Martin Bairstow)*

On 23 September 1989, narrow bodied 141108 is passed in Cottingley Station by 144006. Both are in the West Yorkshire PTE livery. *(Martin Bairstow)*

D246 (later 40046) sweeps round from Churwell towards Morley Low on 29 July 1967 with the 9.15 am (Saturdays only) Leeds to Llandudno. *(M. Mitchell)*

Looking down on Morley Station from above the tunnel. A Leeds to Marsden local accelerates away. *(Martin Bairstow)*

Morley Station lost the booking office in which John Holroyd used to work after the elimination of all staff in August 1985. 47413 passes with a Liverpool to Newcastle express made up of coaches in the blue 'Trans-Pennine' livery on 28 June 1987. *(John Bateman)*

CROWNING
OF BRITAINS
Railway Queen
Belle Vue
ZOOLOGICAL GARDENS
MANCHESTER
SATURDAY SEPTEMBER 26TH.

SPECIAL TRAINS FROM

	NO. 1 TRAIN	NO. 2 TRAIN	ADULTS	CHILDS
LEEDS L.M.S.	12-5	12-30	2/6	1/3
FARNLEY & WORTLEY	12-10	12-35	„	„

Returning from
Manchester EXCHANGE at 9-50 and 10-30p.m.

Fireworks will definitely start at 8.30 p.m. allowing ample time to catch the return train.

CROWNING CEREMONY COMMENCES 4.45 P.M.

Tickets and all information can be obtained from
E. A. Shervington, Pass: Agent, New Stn. LEEDS

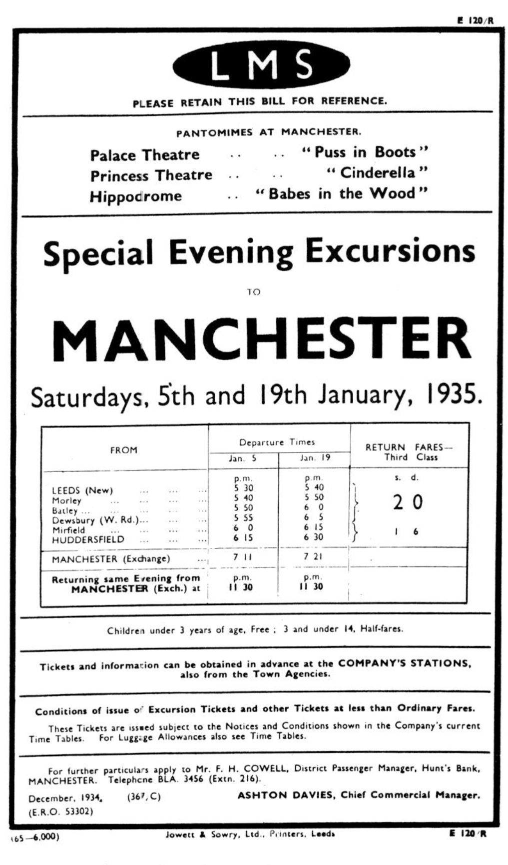

LMS
PLEASE RETAIN THIS BILL FOR REFERENCE.

PANTOMIMES AT MANCHESTER.
Palace Theatre .. .. "Puss in Boots"
Princess Theatre .. .. "Cinderella"
Hippodrome .. "Babes in the Wood"

Special Evening Excursions
TO
MANCHESTER
Saturdays, 5th and 19th January, 1935.

FROM	Departure Times Jan. 5	Jan. 19	RETURN FARES—Third Class
	p.m.	p.m.	s. d.
LEEDS (New)	5 30	5 40	
Morley	5 40	5 50	2 0
Batley	5 50	6 0	
Dewsbury (W. Rd.)...	5 55	6 5	
Mirfield	6 0	6 15	1 6
HUDDERSFIELD	6 15	6 30	
MANCHESTER (Exchange) ...	7 11	7 21	
Returning same Evening from MANCHESTER (Exch.) at	p.m. 11 30	p.m. 11 30	

Children under 3 years of age, Free; 3 and under 14, Half-fares.

Tickets and information can be obtained in advance at the COMPANY'S STATIONS, also from the Town Agencies.

Conditions of issue of Excursion Tickets and other Tickets at less than Ordinary Fares.

These Tickets are issued subject to the Notices and Conditions shown in the Company's current Time Tables. For Luggage Allowances also see Time Tables.

For further particulars apply to Mr. F. H. COWELL, District Passenger Manager, Hunt's Bank, MANCHESTER. Telephone BLA. 3456 (Extn. 216).

December, 1934. (367/C) ASHTON DAVIES, Chief Commercial Manager.
(E.R.O. 53302)

(65—6,000) Jowett & Sowry, Ltd., Printers, Leeds E 120/R

LMS publicity from the 1930s *(David Beeken collection)*

The 17.13 Leeds to Manchester Victoria local formed of a 3 car 'Calder Valley' set starts away from Morley Station and immediately plunges into the 3,369 yard tunnel on 30 May 1984. *(Martin Bairstow)*

An L&Y radial 2-4-2 tank emerging from the Batley end of Morley Tunnel with a Leeds – Huddersfield local in the 1930s. *(D. Ibbotson)*

The Main Line Through Standedge

The First Trans Pennine Railway

Railway communication across the Pennines was established on 1 March 1841 when the Manchester & Leeds Railway completed its circuitous route via the Calder Valley and Normanton, 61 miles in length and involving a journey of 3 hours. In a period of rapid railway expansion this could not long be guaranteed to satisfy public demand for railway facilities. The Manchester & Leeds was a Stephenson line and displayed that engineer's preference for the easiest gradients at the expense not just of an indirect route but of missing some of the more important towns. Dewsbury was afforded a station, later known as Thornhill, more than a mile from the town. The best Huddersfield could get was one at Cooper Bridge, some 3 miles away. A branch line was proposed in 1843 but found little enthusiasm in Huddersfield because the Manchester & Leeds planned to stick to the floor of the valley so as to reach Huddersfield at too low a level to allow for extension onward.

Branch Lines to Stalybridge

The first stage in tracing the development of the Leeds – Huddersfield – Manchester line is to consider how two railways came to arrive in Stalybridge from the Manchester direction.

The Sheffield, Ashton-under-Lyne & Manchester Railway was incorporated on 5 May 1837 to construct what is generally referred to as the Woodhead Line. The first section to open was from a temporary station in Manchester, a forerunner of today's Piccadilly, to Godley on 17 November 1841. One of the intermediate stations was called Ashton but was in fact at Guide Bridge, the nearest point which the main line went to Ashton. Plans for a branch line between Guide Bridge and Stalybridge which would bring the railway through Ashton proper were embodied in an Act of 19 July 1844.

On the same day another Act was passed author ing a different railway from Manchester to Sta bridge. The Ashton, Stalybridge & Liverpool Juncti Railway, a protegé of the Manchester & Leeds, w authorised to build from a junction at Miles Platting a terminus adjacent to that of the SA & MR Stalybridge. The success of the AS & LJ in securi Parliamentary approval despite opposition from t SA & MR may have been due to its ability to give t textile industry in Ashton a direct service to Liverpo thanks to the connection with the Liverpool Manchester Railway at Manchester Victoria. The A & LJ Railway was authorised to amalgamate with t Manchester & Leeds and did so on 9 July 1847, t day the latter changed its name to the Lancashire Yorkshire Railway.

The SA & MR branch from Guide Bridge w delayed by the collapse of a nine arch viaduct Ashton on 19 April 1845 which killed 17 workmen a cost the company £47 4s 6½d in funeral expenses pl £10 to set up a widows and childrens fund. C 23 December 1845 it became the first of the two lin to Stalybridge to be opened. The branch from Mil Platting reached Ashton on 13 April 1846 and w extended to Stalybridge on 5 October of that year.

The Leeds, Dewsbury & Manchester and the Huddersfield & Manchester Railways

These two separate companies were formed provide a direct link between Leeds, Huddersfield a Stalybridge whence they intended to get Manchester by one of the lines just described. T Leeds, Dewsbury & Manchester was authorised 30 June 1845 to build a line from Leeds to Heat Lodge where it would join the Huddersfield Manchester Railway authorised on 21 July of that ye to continue the route to Stalybridge. There w provision in the LD & M Act for it to build the Heat

2-6-4T No. 42355 heads a Leeds – Huddersfield local past Lady Anne Crossing box and under the Great Northern line. In 1893 the LNWR rejected requests for a station at Lady Anne.
(P. Sunderland)

›dge – Huddersfield section if the H & M failed. The & M was further authorised to take over the ıddersfield Canal which crossed the Pennines by eans of a 3 mile tunnel at Standedge. It was hoped at there would be economy in construction if the ilway followed the course of the canal especially at :andedge where the canal could be used to service ork on the railway tunnel.

malgamation Proposals

itially the board of the Huddersfield & Manchester ompany contained representatives of the Sheffield, shton & Manchester Railway and it was expected at this company would take it over. However, whilst e SA & MR shareholders approved such a move the & M proprietors narrowly rejected it on 28 February 346. Another railway which logically might have llen to the SA & MR was the Huddersfield & neffield Junction, authorised in 1845 to build from uddersfield to a junction with the Woodhead Line at enistone. By an Act of 27 July 1846, despite opposi-on from the SA & MR, this line was amalgamated ith the Manchester & Leeds Railway which was ven a strong incentive to get into Huddersfield and ık up with this otherwise unconnected line to enistone.

The Manchester & Leeds realised that there was tle future in being hostile to the proposed eeds – Dewsbury – Huddersfield – Stalybridge – anchester route. It was more important to come to rms with its rival, to get access to Huddersfield, or se its Penistone line would be isolated. Recalling at the M&L desired an independent and direct route to Leeds, it would have made sense for it to have ken over the Leeds, Dewsbury & Manchester Com-ıny and to have incorporated the Leeds – Dewsbury Mirfield line into its own network. Apparently it und the asking price too high and had to forego this oportunity – a decision condemned by Thomas ormington whom we met in *The Manchester & eeds Railway.* Instead, on 9 July 1847, the London & North Western Railway stepped into the vacuum and agreed terms to take over both the Leeds, Dewsbury & Manchester and Huddersfield & Manchester Companies.

It now remained for the LNWR to make a series of agreements with the Manchester & Leeds (itself renamed the Lancashire & Yorkshire Railway). Instead of building a duplicated line from Thornhill to Heaton Lodge, the LNWR was to exercise running powers over the L&Y. In return the latter would enjoy running powers from Heaton Lodge to Huddersfield where a joint passenger station would be provided. The short stretch thence to Springwood Junction, where the Penistone line diverged, would be built jointly. The LNWR would send its Leeds – Manchester trains from Stalybridge to Manchester Victoria over the L&Y Stalybridge branch. The L&Y would be permitted to divert most of its Manchester – Leeds trains through Dewsbury. To come to such a sensible compromise in such a turbulent period may seem remarkable, but the alternatives were to build duplicated lines, to get Parliament to enforce running powers or, in the case of the L&Y, to persevere with a 61 mile Manchester – Leeds route and risk being excluded from Huddersfield.

Opening to Traffic

On 2 August 1847 work has progressed sufficiently to permit passenger services to begin over a single track from Huddersfield to Heaton Lodge. The LNWR established a station just south of the junction at a point not far from the L&Y station at Cooper Bridge so interchange was possible.

The Leeds – Thornhill section was officially opened with due ceremony on Monday 31 July 1848 but appears then to have laid idle until public opening on 18 September from which date the LNWR advertised a Leeds – Huddersfield service.

1 August 1849 saw the opening of the Huddersfield – Stalybridge section and the inauguration of a through service from Leeds Central to Manchester

A 2-6-4T approaches Batley on the LNWR main line as a B1 4-6-0 descends on the adjacent GNR route from Bradford in July 1959. *(P. Sunderland)*

Batley Station has been unstaffed since September 1989 and the building is no longer occupied. *(Martin Bairstow)*

Victoria through Standedge Tunnel. On the same date the LNWR opened its link from Heaton Norris Junction, north of Stockport, to Guide Bridge so that with the help of running powers over the SA & MR Guide Bridge – Stalybridge branch, the Standedge line was connected to the rest of the LNWR network via Stockport.

The Leeds – Manchester route was double track except for Standedge Tunnel itself which was a single bore, 3 miles 66 yards in length and known by the name of its engineer Thomas Nicholson. Movements through the tunnel were regulated by a pilot engine which accompanied each train or the last one in the event of a succession of trains in the same direction – a kind of staff and ticket system. With the build up of traffic, particularly slow freight, Standedge became a bottleneck.

Widening the main line

Work started in 1868 on a second single bore situated to the east of the Nicholson Tunnel. Also named after its engineer, Thomas Nelson of Carlisle, the new tunnel was opened on 12 February 1871. Part way through there is a cross bore, known as the 'cathedral' because of its slightly extravagant architecture, totally wasted since nobody can see it! The 'cathedral' contained a platelayers hut – doubtless a very welcome facility. There is frequent communication between the two tunnels as each linesman's retreat actually cuts through enabling workmen from either side to take refuge from passing trains.

Increasing traffic imposed strains on the capacity of the double track as the LNWR tried to superimpose prestige express passenger workings on the same tracks as slow freights struggling to climb the gradients. From Thornhill LNW Junction through Heaton Lodge and Huddersfield to Springwood Junction there were also L&Y passenger and freight trains competing for paths. Eventually the entire route from Leeds to Stalybridge was increased to four track partly by quadrupling sections of the existing rou and partly through the opening of duplicate lines fro Leeds to Huddersfield and from Diggle to Stalybridg

The LNWR obtained powers to widen its section line and to enlarge Huddersfield station by its Acts 1878 – 1882. Huddersfield Viaduct was widened take five tracks in 1881 – 1883 using stone recovere from Springwood Cutting (between the two tunnel which was enlarged at the same time. Four track were brought into use between Hillhouse and Heato Lodge in April 1884. This work involved a new static at Bradley with four platforms almost entirely und cover.

The L&Y enlarged the Thornhill – Heaton Lodg section to four tracks in 1884 apart from the Cald Bridge at Mirfield which remained with only a doubl line until 1932 much to the annoyance of the LNW who had a much higher proportion of expres passenger traffic passing through this bottleneck tha did its neighbour.

Huddersfield Station was enlarged by the additio of an island platform which opened on 5 June 1886. new roof spanning the enlarged station was unde construction on 10 August 1885 when it collapse killing three workmen. No passengers wer endangered because a Bradford train had departe four minutes earlier and there was nobody under th roof at the moment of impact.

To make way for expanded passenger facilities th former LNWR goods warehouse had to be demo lished. This was replaced by alternative accom modation for both LNW and L&Y Railways a Hillhouse.

10 October 1886 saw the opening of a secon Huddersfield Tunnel, built at joint expense of the tw railways, to give four tracks as far as Springwoo Junction. Quadruple track was extended to Golcar i 1887, and to Slaithwaite in 1890 before reachin Marsden on 1 November 1891.

›e Micklehurst Loop

›cause of engineering difficulties which would have en involved in quadrupling the route from Diggle to alybridge, the LNWR elected instead to build a mpletely separate railway running parallel at no ›re than half a mile distant on the other side of the lley. The Micklehurst Loop opened to goods on ›ecember 1885 and from 3 May 1886, a passenger rvice was provided serving four intermediate ıtions. There were three tunnels on the 6½ mile ›p. Butterhouse (329 yards) was encountered soon ›er Diggle Junction. Royal George was between iezland and Micklehurst whilst Stalybridge New nnel (572 yards) brought the loop back alongside e main line.

ations in Leeds

›ither the Leeds & Selby Railway of 1834 nor the ›rth Midland of 1840 penetrated the centre of Leeds. ıis was achieved in 1846 with the opening of the eds & Bradford Railway and the transfer of Midland ilway traffic to Leeds Wellington Station.

By this time the Railway Mania was in full swing and ur main lines were projected towards Leeds. These, e Leeds Dewsbury & Manchester (later LNWR), anchester & Leeds (L&Y), Leeds & Thirsk (North stern) and Great Northern Railways decided to vest in a common Central Station which would cupy an area to the north of Wellington Street and ›nt onto Park Row. This would have entailed four mpanies sharing a prime site, leaving just the Midland out on a limb at Wellington.

The first of the four lines to open was the Leeds & Dewsbury on 18 September 1848. As no progress had been made with Central Station, emergency facilities were provided on the north side of Wellington Street near to where Central Station was eventually built. During 1849 the Leeds & Thirsk and the Great Northern Railways made similar short term arrangements when their trains began to arrive in Leeds.

From 1 May 1850 one of the Central Station partners, the Leeds & Thirsk transferred its services to Wellington Station and was followed on 1 October by the LNWR on completion of the Copley Hill – Whitehall Junction curve. These moves may have been influenced by frustration at the lack of progress on Central Station but were also due to a realignment of railway politics. The LNWR had joined with the Midland and others in the 'Euston Square Confederacy' which was an alliance aimed against the Great Northern Railway.

Central Station went ahead, albeit on a smaller scale than originally planned, at a site to the south of Wellington Street which left it rather less 'central' than its Midland rival. Two of the joint owners preferred to be tenants of the Midland Railway and did not patronise Leeds Central which was left to the Great Northern and Lancashire & Yorkshire Railways.

In 1869 the LNWR and the North Eastern Railway opened their own joint station at Leeds New, adjacent to Wellington which had become somewhat over worked. Leeds New was a through station as the NER had at the same time built a viaduct to connect it to the Selby line at Marsh Lane.

'Jubilee' class 4-6-0 No. 45654 'Hood' crossing Batley Viaduct with a Hartlepool to Manchester working in July 1962. The Great Northern Dewsbury Loop is in the foreground. *(P. Sunderland)*

The waiting room and toilets on the Huddersfield bound platform at Batley. Photographed in 1965, they have long been demolished. *(John Bateman)*

Class 150/2 Sprinters were introduced in 1987. The 11.20 Holyhead to Hull crossing Batley Viaduct on 21 August that year. *(John Bateman)*

LNWR trains still had to negotiate the very ngested Midland tracks from Whitehall Junction in der to reach their new terminus until 1882. In that ar an independent approach largely on a viaduct ened from Farnley Junction to Canal Junction at e entrance to Leeds. Farnley & Wortley station was sited as all LNWR passenger trains used the new proach into Leeds.

In 1938 the LMS and LNER joined Wellington and ew and called them Leeds City. They insisted, wever, that they could do nothing to end the convenience to through travellers caused by the parate Central Station. At last, in 1957, BR nounced their intention to divert trains from Leeds entral into a remodelled City Station. *Trains ustrated* for May 1959 commented 'No official formation is yet available on the details of the layout organisation involved but in view of the congestion at occurs at the approaches to City Station with its esent flows of traffic at peak travel periods, one agines that it must be fairly drastic'.

Later in 1959, BR detailed their proposal which was involve enlarging the 'New' part of City Station to ecome the sole passenger terminal leaving Wellington for parcels and bringing ex GN trains in by a flyover from Holbeck across the Whitehall Junction complex to descend between the two pairs of ex Midland tracks coming in from Shipley and Ilkley. It was believed that better signalling, cross-overs part way along the through platforms and the elimination of steam would more than compensate for the reduction from 16 to 12 in the number of passenger platforms at Leeds City.

Work began late in 1959 but was stopped in July 1961 by the Government. A fresh go-ahead was received in 1963 for a scaled down scheme without the flyover. As events have turned out this was not critical in that a principal object of the flyover had been to carry passenger trains clear of freight movements on the Midland main line. The proposed Healey Mills type marshalling yard at Stourton, on the Midland south of Leeds, never went ahead and there is now very little freight passing Whitehall Junction.

By means of a new curve at Gelderd Road Junction, trains from Doncaster were given access to the Farnley Viaduct line which was closed to traffic from Huddersfield in December 1966.

All this took place at the height of the Beeching

47460 pauses at Dewsbury Wellington Road on 4 October 1981 with a Newcastle to Liverpool express. It is planned to reinstate one of the centre through lines to provide an overtaking facility here. *(G. W. Morrison)*

period when it was confidently assumed that most local services would be closed and when hourly interval main line services were no more than a dream. The layout of the west end of Leeds station allows practically any manoeuvre to take place but not many all at once. There are four tracks at the most critical point on the canal bridge, where there used to be six and with more passenger trains than ever before, the system is grossly overworked and delays can occur.

Stations in Manchester

Victoria Station, opened on 1 January 1844, was the headquarters of the Lancashire & Yorkshire Railway. Initially it had one through platform with a bay at each end. From July 1844, the LNWR began to use Victoria for its Liverpool trains. When the Standedge line opened in 1849, trains from Leeds entered Victoria over L&Y tracks from Stalybridge and were then able to regain LNWR territory to Liverpool.

As traffic expanded on the two railways, the accommodation at Victoria became inadequate and the station was enlarged progressively. The first extension, in 1855, involved the opening of suburban platforms at the east end for trains to Stalybridge, Oldham and Middleton.

Two new platforms were opened for main line trains in 1865 but were swept away when the station was rebuilt in the late 1870s. A new suburban section with five platforms opened in November 1877. Reconstruction of the main line station with six through platforms was completed in 1884.

At this point the LNWR pulled out of Victoria in favour of its own adjacent Exchange Station. Trains from Leeds via Standedge passed through Victoria on the centre tracks between platforms 11 and 12 in order to reach Exchange. In 1930, platform 11, which is on the original 1844 site was extended to join platform 3 at Exchange. The combined length was 2,238 feet. Exchange closed in 1969 and traffic reverted Victoria to the greater convenience of passengers.

Since May 1989, Trans Pennine services have us Piccadilly. Known for most of its life as Manchest London Road, this station opened on 8 May 1842 replace a temporary structure at Travis Street whi had served for the previous two years. There was o arrival and one departure platform at London Ro with separate booking offices for the Manchester Birmingham and Sheffield, Ashton-Under-Lyne Manchester Railways. These companies becan respectively parts of the LNW and Mancheste Sheffield & Lincolnshire Railways.

The approach to Manchester was widened in 18 giving the MS & LR exclusive use of the pair of trac on the east side of the route together with tv platforms 'numbered' A and B in an enlarged Lond Road Station. In 1882 a platform C was created making a bay in platform B. Electric lighting w installed on the MS & LR side of the station, one of t first public buildings in Manchester to be illuminated. It is claimed that the lamps on platform were shaded to prevent the LNWR from gaining a light from them.

London Road was rebuilt in 1960 and renam Piccadilly in celebration of electrification of the fi part of the route to London. The main station no contains 12 platforms but Trans Pennine Servic going on to Liverpool must use the very congest island platform numbered 13 and 14 which is set at angle from the main station. Opened originally 1 August 1849, the separate 'South Junction' stati was connected by a footbridge to the main station the 1960 rebuilding. In anticipation of the transfer May 1989 of Trans-Pennine and other trains pr viously using Victoria, the 'South Junction' platfor was doubled in length. It is now by far the busiest pa of the station.

40096 crosses the River Calder near Ravensthorpe with a Llandudno to York working on 4 July 1981.
(G.W. Morrison)

A Leeds – Huddersfield local leaves Ravensthorpe and negotiates Thornhill LNW Junction on 30 May 1984.
(Martin Bairstow)

A new style of station architecture at Mirfield.
(Martin Bairstow)

Mirfield Station, complete with overall roof, viewed towards Huddersfield in 1962.
(Peter E. Baughan)

A Metro Cammell set with both cars powered approaching Mirfield on a Huddersfield to Bradford working. The track bed of the Midland branch is on the left and Battyeford Bridge on the right. *(P. Sunderland)*

A class 144 crossing the Calder west of Mirfield in September 1989. *(Martin Bairstow)*

A 'WD' 2-8-0 passing Spen Valley Junction in May 1960. The Leeds New Line branches off to the right of the locomotive. *(P. Sunderland)*

The class 110 'Calder Valley' sets were introduced in 1962 also on services around Huddersfield. In 1983 most sets lost their centre cars. A reduced formation accelerates away from Deighton in the evening of 11 July 1987.
(John Bateman)

'WD' 2-8-0 No. 90123 passing Kirkburton Junction with coal empties in May 1962. This is now the site of Deighton Station. The old station was through the bridge on the Kirkburton branch. *(P. Sunderland)*

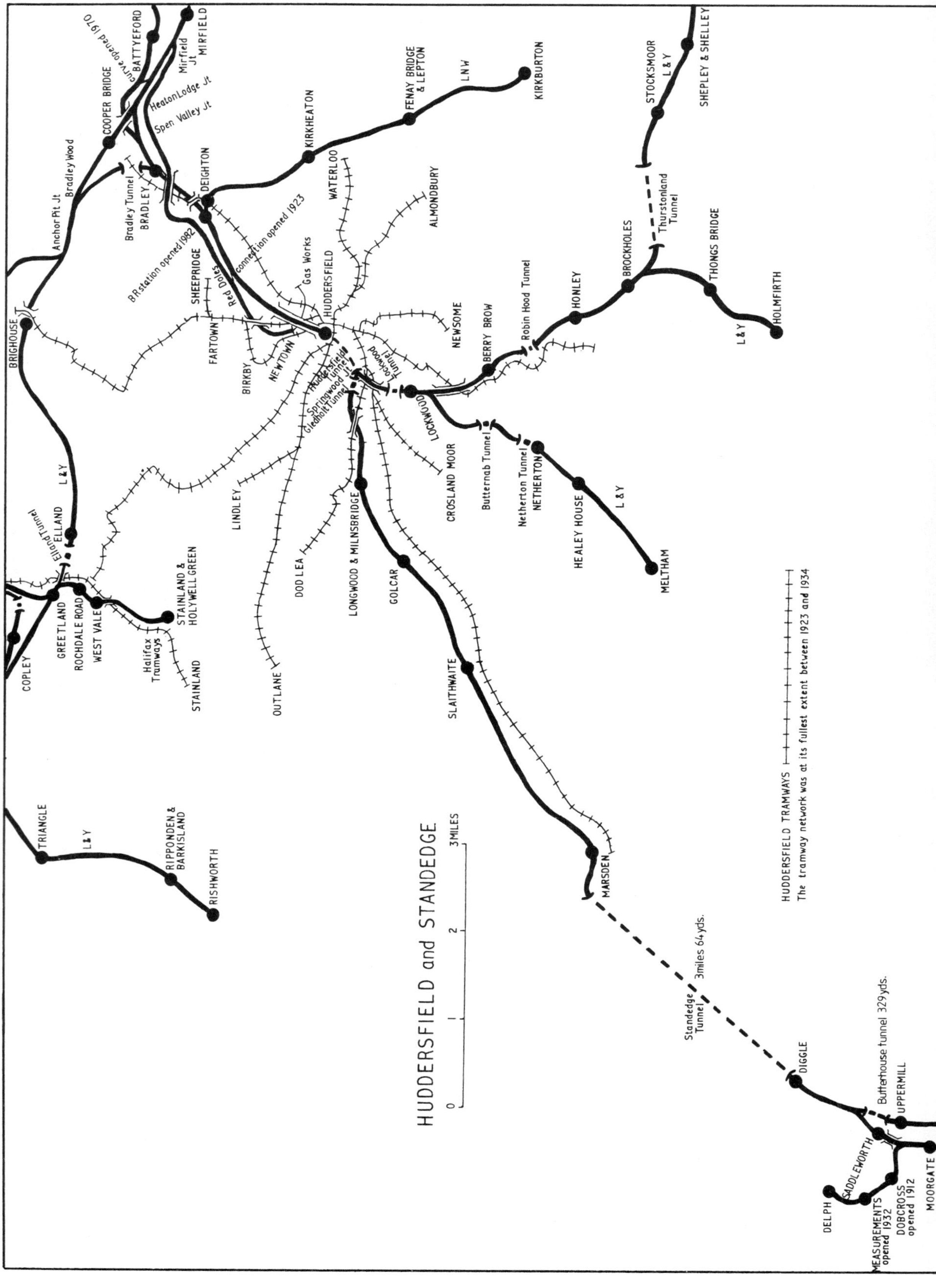
HUDDERSFIELD and STANDEDGE
0
1
2
3 MILES
HUDDERSFIELD TRAMWAYS
The tramway network was at its fullest extent between 1923 and 1934
MIRFIELD
Mirfield Jt
BATTYEFORD
curve opened 1970
COOPER BRIDGE
Heaton Lodge Jt
Spen Valley Jt
Bradley Wood
Anchor Pit Jt
Bradley Tunnel
BRADLEY
DEIGHTON
KIRKHEATON
FENAY BRIDGE & LEPTON
LNW
KIRKBURTON
STOCKSMOOR
L&Y
SHEPLEY & SHELLEY
Thurstonland Tunnel
BROCKHOLES
THONGS BRIDGE
HOLMFIRTH
L&Y
HONLEY
Robin Hood Tunnel
BERRY BROW
NEWSOME
ALMONDBURY
WATERLOO
connection opened 1923
BR station opened 1982
SHEEPRIDGE
Red Doles
Gas Works
HUDDERSFIELD
FARTOWN
BIRKBY
NEWTOWN
Huddersfield Tunnel
Springwood Jt
Gledholt Tunnel
Lockwood Tunnel
LOCKWOOD
CROSLAND MOOR
Butternab Tunnel
Netherton Tunnel
NETHERTON
HEALEY HOUSE
L&Y
MELTHAM
BRIGHOUSE
L&Y
Elland Tunnel
ELLAND
GREETLAND
ROCHDALE ROAD
WEST VALE
STAINLAND & HOLYWELL GREEN
Halifax Tramways
STAINLAND
COPLEY
LINDLEY
OUTLANE
DOD LEA
LONGWOOD & MILNSBRIDGE
GOLCAR
SLAITHWAITE
MARSDEN
Standedge Tunnel
3 miles 64 yds.
DIGGLE
Butterhouse tunnel 329 yds.
UPPERMILL
SADDLEWORTH
DELPH
MEASUREMENTS opened 1932
DOBCROSS opened 1912
MOORGATE
TRIANGLE
L&Y
RIPPONDEN & BARKISLAND
RISHWORTH

45062 comes to a stand at Huddersfield's platform 1 with the 1.22 pm from Newcastle to Liverpool Lime Street on 10 April 1983. Alterations carried out early in 1990 involve widening this platform so as to meet the track on the left of the train but leaving a bay (a revived platform 2) at the nearest end for the Penistone trains. *(G.W. Morrison)*

Standard class 5 No. 73162 passing Hillhouse Shed in May 1962. The motive power depot here dated from 1849 but was enlarged in 1882/3 and again in 1905/6 when it became a through shed. It closed at the end of 1966. *(P. Sunderland)*

'Jubilee' 4-6-0 No. 45708 'Resolution' stands alongside a WD class 2-8-0 at Huddersfield in October 1958 before No. 1 signal box was swept away by the Huddersfield resignalling scheme. *(P. Sunderland)*

'Jubilee' 4-6-0 No. 45558 'Manitoba' emerges from Huddersfield Tunnel and passes Springwood Junction before entering Gledholt Tunnel with a Leeds – Manchester local on 24 May 1959. *(G.W. Morrison)*

Fowler 2-6-4T No. 42343 emerges from Gledholt Tunnel with a Leeds – Stockport local and overtakes Stanier 2-8-0 No. 48743 on a freight on 6 July 1959. *(G. W. Morrison)*

45041 crossing Milnsbridge Viaduct with a Sunday Newcastle to Liverpool in June 1983. *(G. W. Morrison)*

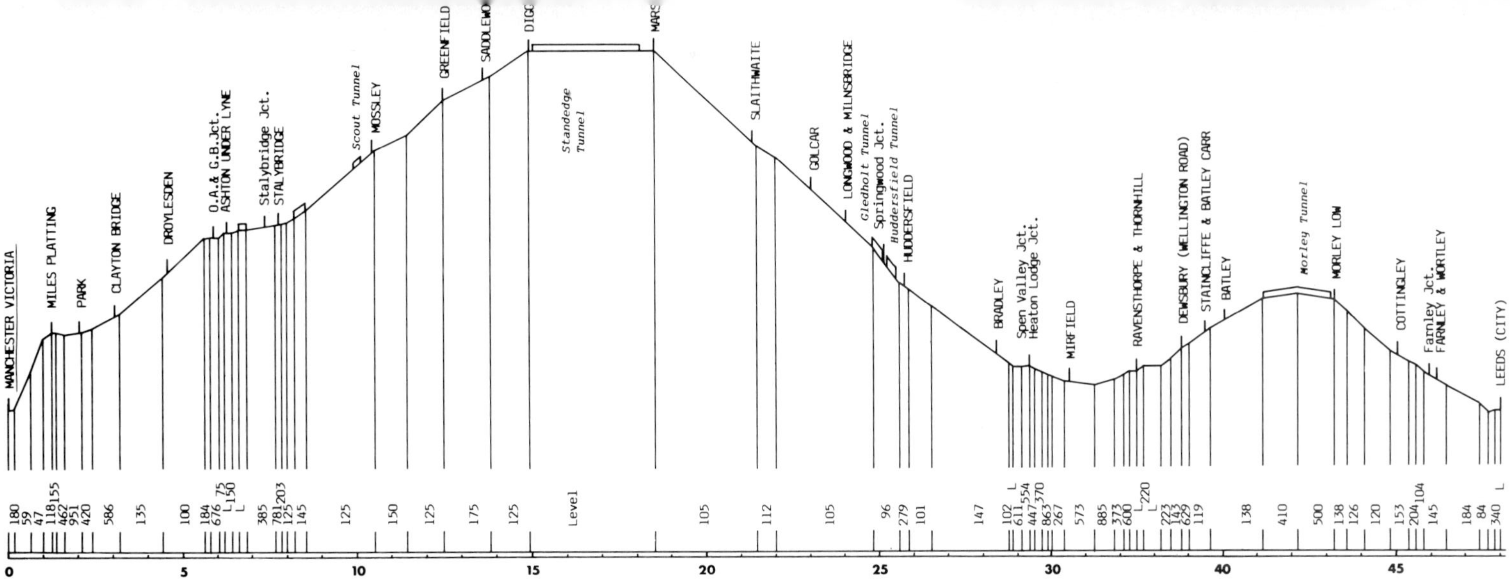

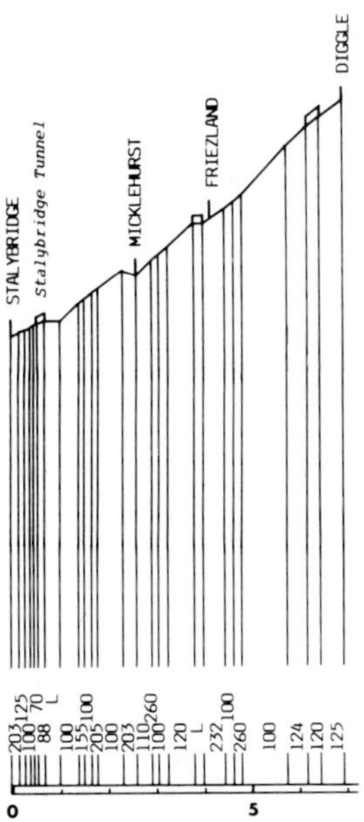

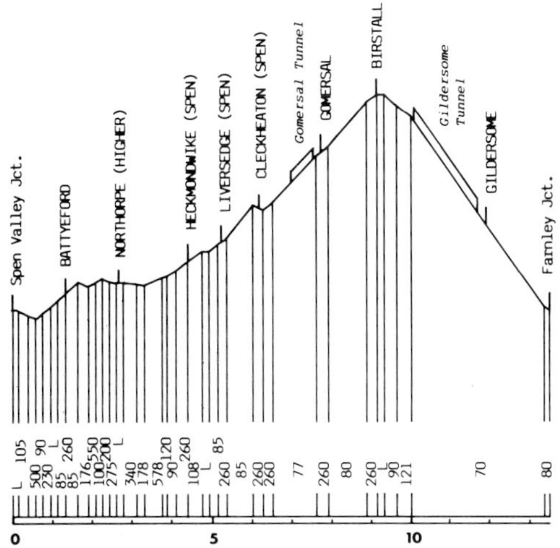

It is not just the gradients but the curvature which restricts the speed of trains. The slewing of two tracks over the previous four track formation has allowed 50 and 55 mph restrictions to be raised. 4P 2-6-4T No. 42406 approaches Marsden with the 4.31 pm from Huddersfield on 27 June 1959. *(D. Butterfield)*

Black five No. 45237 shunts at Longwood goods yard in April 1958. The main yard is off the left of the photograph. *(P. Sunderland)*

'Black Five' No. 44772 of Edge Hill Shed pulls away from Golcar Station with a Leeds to Manchester local on 20 June 1959. *(G.W. Morrison)*

141109 has arrived in the new platform 1 at Marsden on 20 August 1989.
(Martin Bairstow)

56108 negotiates Marsden loop with a 'merry go round' for Fidlers Ferry power station on 19 June 1983. In view of the increase in passenger traffic, most freight has been rerouted onto the Calder Valley line.
(G.W. Morrison)

A 'black five' heads a westbound express into the 'Nelson' Tunnel at Standedge in January 1953.
(Roy Brook)

At the south end of the double-track tunnel, an express emerges behind 45211 on 14 August 1958. The tank supplied water for the troughs just inside this being an appropriate level stretch of line. *(P. Hutchinson)*

LNWR LEEDS-HUDDERSFIELD-MANCHESTER NOV 1850

	WEEKDAYS 3 am	3 am	3 am	3 am	am	3 am	am	3 pm	pm	3 pm	pm	3 pm	pm	pm		SUNDAYS 3 am	3 am	3 pm	3 pm	3 pm	3 pm	
LEEDS WELLINGTON			6 45	8 30	9 30		10 45	12 30	3 15		3 30		5 30	8 15		7 00					6 45	
WORTLEY			6 51	8 36	—		10 51	12 36	—		3 38		5 38	8 23		7 08					6 51	
CHURWELL			6 56	8 42	—		10 57	12 43	—		3 45		5 44	8 29		7 14					6 57	
MORLEY			7 02	8 50	—		11 05	12 49	—		3 51		5 50	8 38		7 20					7 05	
BATLEY			7 10	8 58	—		11 13	12 58	—		4 00		5 59	8 44		7 29					7 14	
DEWSBURY			7 14	9 03	9 50		11 18	1 03	3 35		4 05		6 03	8 48		7 33					7 18	
MIRFIELD			7 23	9 13	10 00		11 28	1 13	3 45		4 15		6 13	8 58		7 43					7 28	
HEATON LODGE			7 28	9 18	—		11 33	1 18	—		4 20		6 18	9 03		7 48					7 33	
BRADLEY			7 34	9 24	—		11 39	1 23	—		4 26		6 22	9 09		7 54					7 39	
HUDDERSFIELD		6 00	7 42	9 32	10 12		11 47	1 30	3 57		4 34		6 30	9 17		8 02					7 45	
LONGWOOD		6 05	—	9 41	—		11 53		—		4 40		6 35	9 23		8 08					7 51	
GOLCAR		6 10	—	9 46	—		11 58		—		4 45		6 40	9 28		8 13					7 56	
SLAITHWAITE		6 15	7 54	9 53	—		12 05		—		4 52		6 47	9 36		8 21					8 04	
MARSDEN		6 20	7 59	10 00	10 30		12 10		4 15		5 00		6 52	9 42		8 26					8 10	
DIGGLE		6 30	8 09		—		12 20		—		5T10		7 02	—		8 36					8 20	
SADDLEWORTH		6 35	8 14		10 45		12 25		4 30		5T15		7 07	9 57		8 42					8 25	
GREENFIELD		6 38	8 20	3	—		12 34	3	—		5T24		7 14	10 04		8 49					8 31	
MOSSLEY		6 46	8 28	am	10T55		12 42	pm	—		5T32		7 21	10 12		8 57					8 39	
STALEYBRIDGE	5 40	6 53	8 35	9 45	11 00	11 40	12 50	2 45	4 45	5 25	5T40	7 10	7 30	10 20		9 05	9 30	2 00	4 30	7 05	8 45	
ASHTON	5 45	—	8 40	9 50	—	11 45	12 55	2 50	—	5 30		7 15	7 35	10 25		9 10	9 35	2 05	4 35	7 10	8 50	
DROYLSDEN	5 50	—	8 45	9 55	—	11 50	1 00	2 55	—	5 35		7 20	—	—		9 15	9 40	2 10	4 40	7 15	8 55	
CLAYTON BRIDGE	5 55	—	8 50	10 00	—	11 55	1 05	3 00	—	5 40		7 25	—	—		9 20	9 45	2 15	4 45	7 20	9 00	
PARK	6 00	—	8 55	10 05	—	12 00	1 10	3 05	—	5 45		7 30	—	—		9 25	9 50	2 20	4 50	7 25	9 05	
MILES PLATTING	6 05	—	9 00	10 10	—	12 05	1 15	3 10	—	5 50		7 35	—	—		9 30	9 55	2 25	4 55	7 30	9 10	
MANCHESTER V	6 10	7 15	9 05	10 15	11 20	12 10	1 20	3 15	5 05	5 55		7 40	7 50	10 40		9 35	10 00	2 30	5 00	7 35	9 15	

	3 am	am	3 am	am	3 am	3 pm	pm	3 pm	pm	3 pm	pm	pm	pm	pm		3 am	3 am	3 am	3 pm	3 pm	3 pm	3 pm
MANCHESTER V	6 30	8 45	9 10	10 30	10 40		2 00	2 05	3 05	4 30	5 00		6 25	8 45		8 10	9 00	10 40	2 30	6 25	8 30	9 30
MILES PLATTING	—	—	9 15	—	10 45		2 05	2 10	—	4 35	—		6 30	8 50		8 15	9 05	10 45	2 35	6 30	8 35	9 35
PARK	—	—	9 20	—	10 50		—	2 15	—	4 40	—		6 35	8 55		8 20	9 10	10 50	2 40	6 35	8 40	9 40
CLAYTON BRIDGE	—	—	9 25	—	10 55		2 11	2 20	—	4 45	—		6 40	9 00		8 25	9 15	10 55	2 45	6 40	8 45	9 45
DROYLSDEN	—	—	9 30	—	11 00		2 15	2 25	—	4 50	—		6 45	9 05		8 30	9 20	11 00	2 50	6 45	8 50	9 50
ASHTON	6 45	9 05	9 35	10 45	11 05		2 20	2 30	3 30	4 55	—		6 50	9 10		8 35	9 25	11 05	2 55	6 50	8 55	9 55
STALEYBRIDGE	6 50	9 10	9 40	10 50	11 10		2 25	2 35	3 35	5 00	5 15	5T50	6 55	9 15		8 40	9 30	11 10	3 00	6 55	9 00	10 00
MOSSLEY	6 58	9 16		10 56			2 33		3 40		—	5T56		9 23		8 48					9 08	
GREENFIELD	7 06	9 24		11 03			2 41		3 45		—	6T03		9 31		8 56					9 16	
SADDLEWORTH	7 12	9 32	3	11 08			2 47		3 50		5 27	6T08		9 37		9 02					9 22	
DIGGLE	7 17	9 37	am	11 13			2 52		3 55		—	6T13		9 42		9 07					9 27	
MARSDEN	7 27	9 47	10 30	11 27			3 02		4 05		5 42	6 30		9 52		9 17					9 37	
SLAITHWAITE	7 33	9 52	10 38	11 32			3 08		4 17		—	6 36		9 58		9 24					9 43	
GOLCAR	7 41	9 58	10 45	11 38			3 15		4 23		—	6 44		10 06		9 32					9 51	
LONGWOOD	7 48	10 02	10 53	11 45			3 18		—		—	6 51		10 13		9 39					9 58	
HUDDERSFIELD	7 54	10 08	11 00	11 52		1 45	3 23		4 33		6 00	6 58		10 19		9 45					10 05	
BRADLEY	8 00	10 13	11 06	11 58		1 53	—		4 39		—	7 04		10 26		9 51					10 11	
HEATON LODGE	8 06	10 18	11 12	12 05		1 59	3 31		4 43		—	7 10		10 32		9 57					10 17	
MIRFIELD	8 11	10 25	11 17	12 10		2 04	3 36		4 47		6 10	7 15		10 37		10 02					10 22	
DEWSBURY	8 21	10 33	11 28	12 19		2 13	3 45		4 56		6 20	7 25		10 47		10 12					10 32	
BATLEY	8 25	10 37	11 33	12 23		2 18	3 49		5 00		—	7 30		10 51		10 16					10 36	
MORLEY	8 32	10 47	11 38	12 33		2 23	3 54		—		—	7 34		11 00		10 25					10 45	
CHURWELL	8 37	10 53	11 44	—		2 28	—		—		—	7 39		11 06		10 31					10 51	
WORTLEY	8 44	10 56	11 50	12 43		2 35	4 02		—		—	7 45		11 12		10 37					10 57	
LEEDS WELLINGTON	8 50	11 00	12 00	12 50		2 45	4 10		5 20		6 40	7 55		11 20		10 45					11 05	

3-conveys third class carriages
T-Tuesdays Thursdays and Saturdays only

Stanier class 5MT 2-6-0 No. 42959 emerging from the single bore 'Nelson' Tunnel at Diggle. *(J. Davenport)*

Train Services

"If the presiding genius who regulates the running of trains between Leeds and Manchester will condescend to introduce a little more regularity into their movements, he would confer a great boon upon the travelling public and promote the cause of religion and good manners by preventing loss of temper and outbreaks of strong language more forcible than elegant. The train due at Marsden at 9.20 in the morning comes, especially on market days, just when and as it happens seemingly regulated by chance; and poor passengers have to stand shivering for an hour together at cold and uncomfortable railway stations, and see other trains whistling past which ought to follow instead of preceding the one they are waiting for with a patience worthy of Job. If the railway authorities cannot make the trains fit in with their time bills, they should make the time bills suit the trains. At all events they ought to fix a time and keep it better than they have done recently."

—Huddersfield Examiner 5 January 1867

The timetable for November 1850, reproduced opposite, shows the service operating when the Standedge route had been opened throughout for just over a year. The local trains between Stalybridge and Manchester were operated by the Lancashire & Yorkshire Railway. It will be noticed that one Leeds bound train and two in the other direction completed the journey in less than two hours. These were not amongst the trains upon which third class passengers were accommodated.

Thirty years later, in 1880, the number of trains had more than doubled. They had also been accelerated. A typical timing was by the 7.45 a.m. from Leeds which, after calling at Batley, Dewsbury, Huddersfield, Greenfield, Stalybridge and Ashton, arrived Manchester Victoria at 9.20. The other way, the 3.50 p.m. from Manchester reached Leeds New at 5.15 with stops only at Stalybridge and Huddersfield. The fastest timing of 1 hour 15 minutes in each direction was achieved by a pair of Mondays only workings. The 7.00 a.m. from Manchester accomplished this with stops at Stalybridge, Huddersfield, Dewsbury and Batley. The return was at10.30 from Leeds with stops only at Huddersfield and Stalybridge. This performance was only a few minutes slower than that being achieved a century later.

Most LNWR trains ran non stop between Ashton Charlestown and Manchester Victoria leaving intermediate stations to be served by the L&Y Stalybridge service. Both companies were in competition with the 15 trains of the Manchester, Sheffield & Lincolnshire Railway which ran each weekday between Stalybridge, Ashton Park Parade and Manchester London Road.

Services in 1910

Another thirty years later and the 1910 timetable reveals a much more comprehensive and complex pattern of service. There are a total of 45 weekday departures from Leeds to Huddersfield in the 'up' (Manchester bound) direction including those routed via the 'New Line'. The first train of the day starts from Saddleworth at the early hour of 5.10. There are sh workings from Huddersfield to Marsden at 5.30 a 6.40. The first train from Leeds is the 5.45 all static to Huddersfield via Heckmondwike followed at 6 by the first service via Dewsbury calling at m stations to arrive Manchester Exchange at 9.10. Th is another slow from Leeds to Manchester at 7.25 b this is overtaken by the 7.55 express calling at Batl Dewsbury, Mirfield and Huddersfield then travelli non stop via the Micklehurst loop to Stalybridge an 9.21 arrival in Manchester.

The 9.20 Hull – Liverpool express leaves Leeds 10.42 and takes only 68 minutes to Manchester w just the stop at Huddersfield. Here passengers c change to the 11.20 for Stockport running non stop Oldham Clegg St then calling at Ashton Oldham Ro 'when required to take up for Macclesfield a beyond'. Timetables of this period are notorious complicated conditional stops. The 4.30 p.m. Hul Liverpool Lime Street, 5.30 from Leeds, calls at Bat 'to take up for Liverpool on the evening previous the opening of the wool sales at Liverpool'. It also ca at Dewsbury for the same reason and in additi 'stops on Fridays when required to take up Greenfield and beyond'.

Saturday night revellers living in the Colne Vall were well catered for with return trains fro Huddersfield to Marsden at 7.47, 8.20, 9.10, 10.(10.30 and 10.55 p.m. The last through train was t 10.40 from Leeds calling at Huddersfield and Sta bridge, where it detached carriages from Newcastle Cardiff, before reaching Manchester at 12.07 a. There were later trains from Leeds to Huddersfield 10.55 Saturdays only via Dewsbury, 11.00 Wedne days and Saturdays only via Heckmondwike a 11.05 every weekday via Dewsbury but this o stopped at Staincliffe on Tuesdays only. None these three trains served Bradley whose citizens cou not stay out in Leeds later than the 9.35 v Heckmondwike if they wished to get home.

Although the Micklehurst Loop carried its full sha of through traffic the intermediate stations were n doing too well. Micklehurst itself closed in 1907 to followed by Staley & Millbrook in 1909. In the 19 timetable there were only four trains booked to stop Uppermill and Friezland. Both the Micklehurst Lo and the Leeds New Line were closed on Sundays was the station at Staincliffe & Batley Carr. The were only 5 Leeds – Manchester trains on Sunda plus one Leeds – Huddersfield and one Huddersfie – Marsden. When staff worked a six day week pl Sundays, if required, it was very convenient for t companies to restrict their operations as much possible on Sundays when demand for travel was any case rather limited.

The First World War and After

As the twentieth century entered its second deca there had been relative stability in Europe for almc 100 years. In that time there had been a comple ınsformation from a medieval to an industrial onomy and this had brought a gradual advance in e standard of living of most people but there was a ge gap between the handful upon whom wealth is concentrated and the masses who were kept very ıch in their place. The Railway Industry was mbolic of this well ordered, advancing if not entirely t, society and, despite rumblings of discontent ch as the 1911 strike there was no reason right up to August 1914 to suppose that things would not ntinue to develop according to the established ttern. The West Riding Lines of the Midland mbolise the way the railway companies were still inking. Then suddenly the failure of politicians in itain, France and Germany to deal with what was no ore than the latest in a succession of Balkan crises ınged Europe into a holocaust.

As the war which would be 'over by Christmas' ent into its third year, the Executive Committee ntrolling the railways on behalf of the Government dered cuts in passenger services including the emporary' closure of some stations and branch lines. e remaining stopping services on the Micklehurst op ceased at the end of 1916, permanently as it rned out. A number of smaller stations were closed ring 1917 in order to free railway staff to join in the rnage in Flanders. Churwell and Staincliffe did wever reopen after the war.

Having regained their independence the railways re compulsorily amalgamated under the 'grouping'. The London & North Western Railway merged with the Lancashire & Yorkshire on 1 January 1922, twelve months before becoming part of the London Midland & Scottish Railway. This organisation faced increasing pressure for better pay and conditions at the same time that it began to feel the effect of competition from the then unregulated bus and lorry operations which sprang up on a large scale during the 1920s. Of course, provided that the overall demand for transport increases, a drop in the railways' relative share of the market does not necessarily entail an absolute reduction in the volume of rail traffic. What it does mean is a change in the type of traffic carried with new opportunities to replace those traditional movements which may find road transport more suitable.

Just how far the LMS moved towards adapting to new conditions, at least on its 'Trans-Pennine' services, is demonstrated by the 1938 timetable which bears a remarkable similarity to its pre First World War counterpart.

Ten years later the first BR timetable reveals the effect of the Second World War, coal shortages and general austerity. The number of trains leaving Leeds for Huddersfield is down to 32 and the fastest Leeds – Manchester timing is 78 minutes, compared with 70 minutes in 1938.

Individual station closures took place on a piecemeal basis. Churwell had closed during the war, Bradley succumbed in 1950. Staincliffe followed in

A Leeds to Belle Vue excursion passing Diggle behind ex LNWR 7F 0-8-0 No. 49367. *(J. Davenport)*

Stanier 8F 2-8-0 No. 48692 brings an eastbound freight off the Micklehurst Loop at Diggle Junction in August 1958. The guards van has just passed through Butterhouse Tunnel. *(P. Hutchinson)*

1952 as did Farnley & Wortley. These stations were, of course, staffed up to closure. It was at least another thirty years before the principle of guards issuing tickets was generally accepted.

Dieselisation

January 1961 saw something of a revolution with the introduction of an hourly interval diesel service replacing the less frequent steam trains between Leeds, Manchester and Liverpool. There were four through trains from Newcastle in place of the previous three and these were hauled by class 40 locomotives. The remainder, including a number starting from Hull, were worked by purpose built six car diesel multiple units. These incorporated a griddle type buffet amongst the four powered and two trailer cars making up each 1,840 hp formation. Both compartment and open seating was on offer and first class passengers were afforded a forward view through the driving cab at both ends of the set.

The 'Trans-Pennine' dmus were able to reduce the Leeds – Manchester timing down to 68 minutes stopping at Huddersfield and Stalybridge and travelling initially via the Spen Valley to avoid the risk of signal checks in the congested Mirfield and Heaton Lodge area. By contrast the loco hauled trains were a bit of a disappointment. The 2,000 hp engines weighing 133 tons themselves could not match the dmu performance with a ten coach load and therefore ha to miss station stops in order to conform as nearly a possible to the hourly interval timetable betwee Leeds and Liverpool. The North Eastern Region of B had considered whether a time of 60 minutes betwee Leeds and Manchester could be achieved but ha concluded that the expense of even higher powere dmus and the easing of speed restrictions along th route would not be justified at a time when 'the seemed little prospect that rival means of transpo across the Pennines would offer faster travel in th next few years' (*Trains Illustrated* April 1961).

Local journeys between Leeds and Huddersfie were catered for by a dmu operating at hour intervals and continuing to Manchester about eve two hours.

These changes came on the eve of the Beechin Report under which the local stations betwee Huddersfield and Manchester were listed for closur No decision was made by the Minister of Transpo until 1968. Longwood, Golcar, Slaithwaite, Diggl Saddleworth, Droylsden and Clayton Bridge we closed in October that year but Marsden, Greenfiel Mossley and Park were retained with their servic virtually reduced to peak hours only. Greenfield an Mossley were closed on Saturdays as well as Sunda until the late 1970s.

A threat to close Morley, Batley and Ravensthorp Stations was lifted in 1969 but the stopping servic

47436 climbing between Saddleworth and Diggle with the 15.05 Bangor to Scarborough service on 4 July 1983. *(G. W. Morrison)*

A Leeds – Manchester local crossing Saddleworth Viaduct behind 'black five' No. 45409. *(J. Davenport)*

between Leeds and Huddersfield was reduced back to austerity levels.

In pre-Beeching times, where a passenger service was withdrawn, it had usually been the practice to retain goods facilities so that even Micklehurst, which closed in 1907, still received the odd wagon of coal until 1964. That was the sort of operation which Dr Beeching was particularly keen to see removed and during the 1960s many small goods yards closed. The process has continued since so that there are virtually no public goods depots left.

Closure of the local yards together with a reduction in slow freight movements along the main line permitted the closure of the Micklehurst Loop and also allowed the two single line tunnels at Standedge to be taken out of use.

As recorded in *The Sheffield, Ashton Under Lyne & Manchester Railway* it was *Modern Railways* for September 1964 which carried the first report of the proposed segregation of passenger and freight traffic between Sheffield and Manchester. This led to the withdrawal of passenger trains over the Woodhead Line in 1970 followed by complete closure of that route 11 years later. The same report predicted a similar happening between Leeds and Manchester whereby the Standedge Line would lose its passenger service in favour of the Calder Valley. This has never come remotely near to a serious suggestion.

On the contrary, by the late 1960s, BR was convinced that there would be heavy freight traffic passing through Heaton Lodge 'bottleneck' on the Calde Valley route from Healey Mills towards Sowerb Bridge but the passenger trains would all be goin from Leeds to Huddersfield and beyond. To separat these conflicting movements, they created a dive under at Heaton Lodge using the formation of th Leeds New Line to get under the Calder Valley tracks

By 1968, BR complacency over Trans-Pennin journey times was at least being brought into questio by the imminent completion of the M62 motorway. I those days, it was a sign of dynamic management t propose a cut in railway services which nobody els had thought of. The November issue of *Moder Railways* applauded the elimination of Huddersfiel stops from the schedules of two Newcastle t Liverpool trains in each direction. Under the headin 'Huddersfield cuts are a pointer' it welcomed 'the firs steps to cut losses on the Trans-Pennine service b concentrating on the more remunerative sectors o the market. Inevitably, the less promising areas wi get a poorer deal: and the significant sufferer i Huddersfield'. 'Such places as York (!), Hull an Huddersfield' were dismissed as 'towns with n growth potential which impede the attack on promis ing long distance markets'. The same editorial di however concede one flaw in the argument for non stop Leeds – Manchester trains. The trains concerne were actually slower than Trans-Pennine dmus callin at both Huddersfield and Stalybridge because of th inadequacy of the class 40 locomotives.

Rebuilt 'patriot' 4-6-0 No. 45535 'Sir Herbert Walker KCB' passing Greenfield on the 9 am Liverpool Lime Street to Newcastle express. *(J. Davenport)*

A threat which was not lifted until 1974 involved the roposed withdrawal of the Stalybridge to Stockport ervice, used by travellers from Leeds and 'uddersfield direction to connect with trains for rewe, the West Midlands, South and Mid Wales. Vhilst local patronage was fairly poor, many users of ie connecting service were going long distance robably with luggage. BR was apparently prepared) deposit them at Manchester Victoria and let them nd their own way to Piccadilly Station a mile away. ortunately the service was one of six outstanding losure cases which the Minister of Transport nnounced would be dropped at the beginning of 974 in a move which more or less marked the end of ny decline in the size of the rail network.

A significant change in the pattern of both main line nd local services occured in May 1979. The ıtroduction of high speed trains on the East Coast lain Line permitted the transfer of class 45 and 47 ›comotives and Mark 2 coaches on to the Trans-ennine route. An hourly service was offered etween York and Liverpool taking 66 minutes for the eeds – Manchester journey with three stops. Four ains continued to start from Newcastle but Hull was ɪft with only a connecting dmu. From January 1982, ıost of the trains starting from York were extended ack to Scarborough. In May 1983 alternate trains vere diverted to North Wales rather than Liverpool.

Also in 1979, the West Yorkshire PTE sponsored the reintroduction of an hourly Leeds – Huddersfield local service with alternative trains extended to Marsden. Three years later the Greater Manchester PTE was persuaded to support the continuation of a few trains from Marsden to Manchester. 1982 also saw two stations rebuilt at the expense of the West Yorkshire PTE. In view of the commitment to run trains to Marsden, the reopening of Slaithwaite was a logical development. More surprising was Deighton situated a few yards from its predecessor on the Kirkburton branch which had booked its last passenger in 1930. A further station was opened in April 1988 at Cottingley where a housing estate has developed near to the site of Churwell Station which had closed in 1940.

The 'Sprinter' Revolution

In the 1980s the Trans-Pennine railway faced competition from both private cars and deregulated buses driving along a motorway built and maintained at the expense of the tax payer. Rolling stock was in need of replacement and there was pressure from the Government for a reduction in subsidies.

The BR response, somewhat in contrast to earlier defeatist policies, was for a new generation of trains with higher acceleration operating more frequently over tracks which have had many of the worst speed restrictions removed.

For years the subway at Greenfield (entrance in foreground) was subject to flooding. It was eventually replaced in 1977 by a genuine LNWR footbridge albeit with a number of fibreglass replacement castings. A Trans-Pennine unit passes on the 14.02 Leeds to Manchester on 24 September. *(Larry Goddard)*

56023 descending towards Mossley with a 'merry go round' coal train from Healey Mills to Fidlers Ferry, near Warrington, on 17 June 1983. *(G. W. Morrison)*

May 1987 saw a new timetable with half hourly expresses on the Leeds to Manchester section of the Trans-Pennine route. From York to Liverpool, there was a train every hour comprising alternately a 'Sprinter' dmu from Scarborough and a class 47 hauled train from Newcastle. These stopped at Huddersfield and Stalybridge completing the Leeds – Manchester journey in 62 minutes. The other hourly train was a 'Sprinter' from Hull to Chester or beyond and this stopped at Dewsbury and Huddersfield.

The elusive 60 minute schedule was achieved in the May 1988 timetable thanks largely to the remodelling of Thornhill LNW and Heaton Lodge Junctions. There was also a further improvement in the local service with a train from Leeds to Marsden every hour on weekdays and every two hours on Sundays. For the first time all stations on the West Yorkshire side of Standedge Tunnel were open seven days per week. An additional Leeds to Huddersfield local was introduced each hour on Saturdays.

The first 'Sprinters' on the Trans-Pennine service were of the class 150/2 variety. They drew criticism that they were less comfortable than the previous loco hauled stock but from early 1989 they began to be replaced by 'Super Sprinters' of class 156. These offer a mixture of seating bays with tables and rows of so called aircraft style seats all facing the same directio They have no first class accommodation. Each tw car set has one 'superloo' with air operated doors an locking mechanism. Two emergency brake handle are placed within easy reach and the train is liable come to an abrupt halt whenever one of these is use in the belief that it will either open the door or flush th toilet.

Revised Arrangements in Manchester

Until May 1989, Manchester was served by tw virtually separate rail systems based on Piccadilly an Victoria Stations. The former had benefited fro modernisation in the 1960s when the route t London was electrified. By contrast the lines radiatin from Victoria have long presented a very run dow appearance. The development of traffic north c Manchester was restricted by the one mile walk or bu ride which faced any travellers who might wish t continue their journeys from Piccadilly. Passenge from the Standedge Line were actually amongst th least disadvantaged because they did have th Stalybridge – Stockport facility.

Under the new arrangements, trains fro Newcastle and Scarborough to Liverpool take th

·mer Great Central route from Stalybridge to ınchester Piccadilly continuing to Liverpool via arrington Central. The hourly trains from Hull follow ; same route but terminate at Piccadilly. They no ıger go through to North Wales.

The concentration of all main line trains on one ıtion in Manchester poses two main problems. One pressure on the South Junction line through ıtforms 13 and 14 at Piccadilly. The other is that rvices remaining at Victoria are even more isolated an before. To help relieve both these situations the ıester and North Wales trains continue to use ctoria. They now start from Stalybridge giving nnections into and out of the Scarborough and ·wcastle trains. The Hull trains do not stop at alybridge.

The Huddersfield to Manchester local service was proved in the May 1989 timetable to give a better ·quency during the morning and evening peaks but th long gaps during the day time. These trains go to ctoria serving Ashton-Under-Lyne.

ıture Plans

ıe May 1990 timetable should see the Leeds – ıddersfield – Manchester Piccadilly service increased to three expresses per hour. A loco hauled train will run hourly from Newcastle to Liverpool whilst class 156 'Sprinters' will link both Scarborough and Hull with Manchester every hour. It was hoped that all these workings would be in the hands of air conditioned 90 mph 'Sprinters' of class 158 but their delivery has been delayed. When they do arrive it is intended that the Newcastle service may revert to two hourly with the alternate train starting instead at Middlesbrough. The Hull train should run through to Manchester Airport when that branch opens in 1993.

It is also planned from May 1990 for the Stalybridge to North Wales train to start back from Wakefield Westgate serving all stations to Ashton in place of local trains.

Electrification remains a long term possibility. 'Trans-Pennine' trains already run 'under the wires' between Newcastle and Colton Junction (south of York), from Guide Bridge to Deansgate and from Allerton to Liverpool Lime Street.

The West Yorkshire PTE proposes a resumption of passenger traffic along the Calder Valley Line through Brighouse. It is not yet clear what form this reopening would take – whether a Leeds – Dewsbury – Halifax service or an extension of the Sheffield – Penistone – Huddersfield trains to Halifax.

40196 climbing down from Mossley towards Greenfield with a freight composed entirely of traditional short 4 wheel wagons on the evening of 1 July 1981. *(Larry Goddard)*

Mossley Station viewed towards Huddersfield in 1968. The 1990 timetable should give Mossley a better service. *(G.C. Lewthwaite)*

46036 climbing past the cooling towers of Tame Valley power station between Stalybridge and Mossley with the 15.10 Liverpool – Newcastle on 3 August 1977. The power station, since demolished, was served from the Micklehurst Loop. *(Larry Goddard)*

The Micklehurst Loop. Ex-LNW 7F 0-8-0 No. 9020 passing Uppermill with a Leeds bound freight in the late 1940s. *(J. Davenport)*

Ex War Department 8F 2-8-0 No. 90671 passing Uppermill with the 17.55 freight from Diggle to Heaton Norris (Stockport). *(J. Davenport)*

Un-named 'Patriot' class 4-6-0 No. 45550 passing Uppermill with a St Helens to Wakefield rugby special. *(J. Davenport)*

Fowler 7F 0-8-0 No. 49662 passing Micklehurst with southbound freight. *(J. Davenport)*

Stanier 8F 2-8-0 No. 48522 passing Micklehurst with a northbound freight. *(J. Davenport)*

Standard class 5 No. 73162 takes the Micklehurst Loop as it pulls away from Stalybridge with a Huddersfield bound freight. *(P. Sunderland)*

The 2.04 pm Macclesfield to Manchester Piccadilly leaving Fairfield for Droylsden Station on 1 August 1963. The northernmost pair of tracks (on the right) have been lifted but could eventually be relaid as part of the Manchester Light Metro system. *(Peter E. Baughan)*

After their displacement from the Standedge line in 1979, the 'Trans Pennine' units were made into hybrid 4-car formations with Swindon cross country sets. A Manchester Piccadilly to Sheffield express passes Ashburys on 3 April 1982. That service would now go via Stockport. *(Martin Bairstow)*

Class 304 electrics on the Alderley Edge to Altrincham services pass in platforms 13 and 14 on the 'South Junction' line at Manchester Piccadilly. This part of the station is now extremely busy. *(Martin Bairstow)*

Underneath the main train shed at Piccadilly stands one of the d.c. units which worked the Glossop and Hadfield route before conversion to a.c. in 1984. *(Martin Bairstow)*

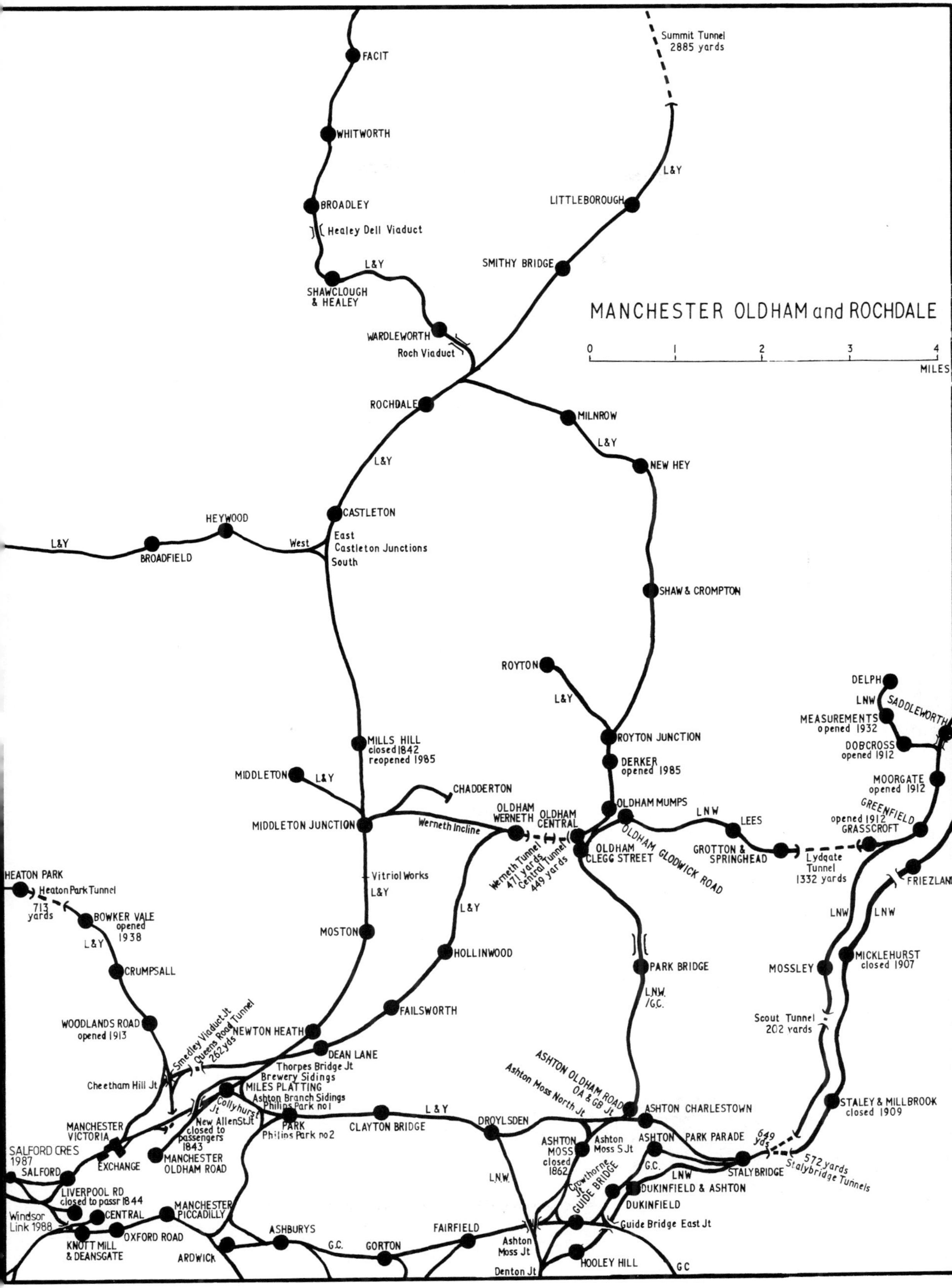
MANCHESTER OLDHAM and ROCHDALE
0 1 2 3 4
MILES
Summit Tunnel
2885 yards
FACIT
WHITWORTH
BROADLEY
Healey Dell Viaduct
L&Y
SHAWCLOUGH & HEALEY
WARDLEWORTH
Roch Viaduct
LITTLEBOROUGH
SMITHY BRIDGE
ROCHDALE
MILNROW
NEW HEY
CASTLETON
HEYWOOD
BROADFIELD
West
East
Castleton Junctions
South
SHAW & CROMPTON
ROYTON
ROYTON JUNCTION
DERKER
opened 1985
MILLS HILL
closed 1842
reopened 1985
MIDDLETON
CHADDERTON
MIDDLETON JUNCTION
Werneth Incline
OLDHAM WERNETH
OLDHAM CENTRAL
OLDHAM MUMPS
OLDHAM CLEGG STREET
OLDHAM GLODWICK ROAD
Werneth Tunnel 471 yards
Central Tunnel 449 yards
LNW
LEES
GROTTON & SPRINGHEAD
Lydgate Tunnel
1332 yards
DELPH
SADDLEWORTH
MEASUREMENTS
opened 1932
DOBCROSS
opened 1912
MOORGATE
opened 1912
GREENFIELD
opened 1912
GRASSCROFT
FRIEZLAND
HEATON PARK
Heaton Park Tunnel
713 yards
BOWKER VALE
opened 1938
CRUMPSALL
Vitriol Works
MOSTON
HOLLINWOOD
FAILSWORTH
PARK BRIDGE
LNW. /GC.
MOSSLEY
MICKLEHURST
closed 1907
Scout Tunnel
202 yards
WOODLANDS ROAD
opened 1913
Smedley Viaduct Jt
Queens Road Tunnel
262 yds
NEWTON HEATH
DEAN LANE
Thorpes Bridge Jt
Brewery Sidings
MILES PLATTING
Ashton Branch Sidings
Philips Park no1
Cheetham Hill Jt
Collyhurst Jt
New Allen St Jt
closed to passengers 1843
MANCHESTER OLDHAM ROAD
MANCHESTER VICTORIA
EXCHANGE
SALFORD CRES
1987
SALFORD
PARK
Philips Park no2
CLAYTON BRIDGE
DROYLSDEN
ASHTON OLDHAM ROAD
OA & GB Jt
Ashton Moss North Jt
ASHTON CHARLESTOWN
STALEY & MILLBROOK
closed 1909
ASHTON MOSS
closed 1862
Ashton Moss S Jt
ASHTON
PARK PARADE
649 yds
572 yards
Stalybridge Tunnels
STALYBRIDGE
Crowthorne Jt
GUIDE BRIDGE
G.C.
DUKINFIELD & ASHTON
DUKINFIELD
Guide Bridge East Jt
LIVERPOOL RD
closed to passr 1844
CENTRAL
Windsor Link 1988
KNOTT MILL & DEANSGATE
OXFORD ROAD
MANCHESTER PICCADILLY
ARDWICK
ASHBURYS
GORTON
FAIRFIELD
Ashton Moss Jt
Denton Jt
HOOLEY HILL
GC

'Jubilee' class 4-6-0 No. 45678 'De Robeck' restarts a Leeds – Manchester semi-fast from Ashton Charlestown. *(J. Davenport)*

Hughes/Fowler 'crab' 2-6-0 No. 42766 passing Droylsden with a Manchester Exchange to Leeds semi-fast. The station here had platforms also on the line curving towards Stockport. *(J. Davenport)*

The 11.05 Liverpool Lime Street to Scarborough crossing Droylsden Viaduct behind 47557 on 11 September 1982. *(G.W. Morrison)*

A class 40-hauled Newcastle to Liverpool Lime Street express passes through Manchester Victoria on its way to Exchange Station in June 1961. 4-6-0 No. 45205 stands in platform 12. *(P. Sunderland)*

A North Wales express leaving Manchester Exchange on 17 March 1954 behind class 4P compound 4-4-0 No. 40925. *(B.K.B. Green)*

The Leeds New Line

A Fowler 2-6-4T climbs away from Farnley Junction with a train from Leeds to Huddersfield via the 'New' line in February 1959. It is crossing over the 'old' line. *(P. Sunderland)*

The duplicate route from Huddersfield to Leeds opened by the LNWR in 1900 achieved three main purposes. It effectively completed quadruple track all the way from Stalybridge to Leeds, it avoided the 'bottleneck' in the Heaton Lodge/Thornhill area and it improved communications in the Spen Valley.

Henry Oakley, the Great Northern General Manager, described it as an annual event to receive a delegation from the Spen Valley who would express dissatisfaction at the service provided by the Lancashire & Yorkshire Railway and implore the GNR to build an extension into the area. By 1881 the GNR appeared set to seek powers for a branch it had surveyed which would begin with a triangular junction near Batley Carr and run to Cleckheaton by way of Heckmondwike and Liversedge. This would have connected the Spen Valley towns to Wakefield Westgate and, on the completion of the GNR Batley – Beeston branch, could have offered a direct service to Leeds, the facility the Spen Valley people seemed to want the most.

The L&Y took the threat seriously and in 1882 came to an agreement with the GN whereby duplicate construction would be avoided in favour of some short connections and a mutual exchange of running powers. This satisfied the GN who in 1886 opened the 1¼ mile link between Hare Park and Crofton Junctions, south of Wakefield. This permitted trains from their main line to enter Wakefield Kirkgate and then run over the L&Y through Thornhill, the Spen Valley and then on to Halifax, courtesy of the Low Moor south curve which was provided by the L&Y under the 1882 agreement.

Another product of GN/L&Y co-operation involved new construction in the Pudsey and Dewsbury areas leading eventually to a joint circular service between Leeds and the Spen Valley. This did not materialise until 1893 by which time patience in the Spen Valley had run out. Disappointment with the GN had caus the annual delegations to be redirected towards t LNWR headquarters at Euston.

The LNWR considered quadrupling its existi route from Thornhill to Leeds but foresaw problem finding room in the Batley area where its line was close to that of the GNR that there was no room f widening. Building a second tunnel at Morley wou have been difficult because of mining operatio which had already caused considerable damage to t existing tunnel. (In later years it took from 1920 1932 to repair and reline 1,400 yards of the tunne Even if the Thornhill – Leeds stretch could have be quadrupled the LNWR would have been left with t bottleneck from Heaton Lodge to Thornhill.

Therefore in 1891 the LNWR tried unsuccessfully promote a bill for a new railway from Spen Vall Junction, north of Bradley, via Heckmondwike a Cleckheaton to rejoin the Dewsbury line at Farnl Junction. The Bill was reintroduced in 1892. The ma changes were the inclusion of plans for a flyi junction at Farnley and the substitution of a cutting f the 580 yard tunnel which had been proposed Heckmondwike. The L&Y pleaded that the proje should be restricted to the Cleckheaton – Lee section and that the existing L&Y Spen Valley li should be made available to LNWR trains betwe Mirfield and Cleckheaton. The LNWR argued that th would defeat the object which was to avoid Heat Lodge and Mirfield. The Bill, which had a lot of loc support, received Royal Assent on 27 June 1892.

Contracts for the construction of the new railw were not let until 1895. Prior to that arrangements h been made to rehouse people whose homes were be demolished. 80 new houses were built at Hec mondwike and 12 at Battyeford. Work took longer complete than anticipated and the target date of 18 passed. In September 1899 it was possible to beg eight operation over the southern extremity of the ute as far as Northorpe. The line opened throughout 1 October 1900.

Trains taking the 'New Line' left the old route pposite Farnley Junction loco shed and began the 1 70 climb on an embankment passing over Gelderd oad near the Pack Horse Inn and then crossing over e Dewsbury line before coming alongside the down ne. The flying junction was a clever piece of ngineering which not only avoided conflicting movements but allowed up trains to start the climb from rther back. The down line dropped more quickly at 1 52 to reach the level of the Dewsbury route before assing the engine shed.

The steady climb at 1 in 70 continued for the first ½ miles to beyond Gildersome Tunnel. The station Gildersome was forced by the tunnel to be sited ome distance from the town which was much better erved by the Great Northern Railway. The situation as parallel to that at Morley but much worse. The NWR station became a temporary war time casualty om 1 August 1917 but it reopened on 5 May 1919 nly to close permanently on 9 July 1921.

The line reached a summit before Upper Birstall. ere the wooden station stood on an embankment on e west side of Gelderd Road. It was renamed Birstall own in 1935 presumably to try and raise the profile of e LMS in Birstall. A falling gradient brought the ilway to Gomersal, another wooden structure set on n embankment west of the bridge over Bradford oad. The goods shed here was larger than at other ations on the line because it took over an existing uilding previously used as a textile mill.

The second major tunnel was reached immediately on leaving the station area at Gomersal. 819 yards in length it brought the line into the Spen Valley. The site for Cleckheaton Station was achieved by creating a ledge on the hillside and then by providing a road viaduct to connect it to the town which was more than ½ mile away across the valley. As at Liversedge and Heckmondwike, the suffix 'Spen' was added in early LMS days to distinguish the ex LNWR station from the one on the parallel L&Y route which became 'Central'. At Cleckheaton this was certainly appropriate.

The journey through the Spen Valley was mostly on a falling gradient at a maximum of 1 in 85. Liversedge was another wooden station. The 'up' and 'down' platforms were served by separate covered staircases from Listing Lane which the railway crossed by a bridge at the north end of the station.

The railway approached Heckmondwike through a cutting which was crossed in quick succession by no fewer than seven overbridges including the 50 yard tunnel under Bridge Street. Passengers entered the station through two separate archways on the High Street bridge at the south end from which staircases led down to the platforms which were built of brick. In LNWR days there was a bay at the Leeds end of the down platform but track was removed from this when the station signal box was closed about 1920.

Because of the cramped nature of the station area, the goods facilities were provided further on just before the bridge over the L&Y Ravensthorpe branch. There was a further signal box here called Heckmondwike Goods. The railway crossed over the

'Jubilee' 4-6-0 No. 45649 'Hawkins' heads the 12.35 pm Leeds – Manchester through Gildersome East on 6 July 1961. *(G.W. Morrison)*

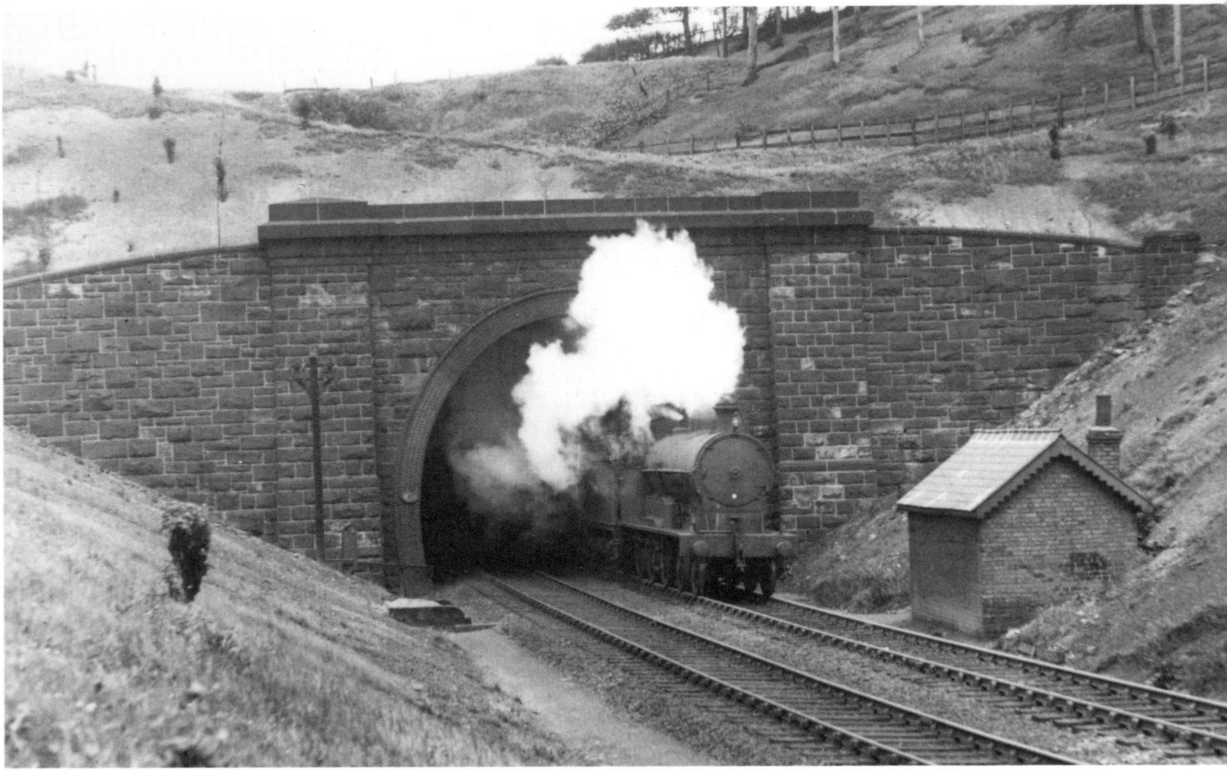

An ex LNWR 4-6-0 'Claughton' emerging from Gildersome Tunnel with a Huddersfield train in the early 1930s. *(D. Ibbotson)*

River Spen by means of Heckmondwike Viaduct, 80 yards in length compromising steel girders supported by brick arches. There then followed a bridge over the L&Y Heckmondwike to Mirfield branch.

Prior to 1921, Northorpe Station stood on the embankment at the Leeds side of the bridge over Shillbank Lane. It was built in the familiar wooden style with separate covered staircases leading up from the roadway to the two platforms. On the evening of 11 July 1921, an embankment fire was started by a spark from an engine just beyond the Leeds end of the station. Following a spell of very hot weather the grass was very dry as was the woodwork of the station. Fanned by a gentle breeze the fire soon took hold and engulfed the station which was almost completely destroyed. Traffic was suspended for two days whilst damage to the track was made good. A replacement station was built, again in wood, adjacent to the goods yard on the Huddersfield side of Shillbank Lane. In 1924 to avoid confusion with the nearby ex L&Y station at Northorpe North Road, the LMS applied the suffix 'Higher' to the ex LNW establishment.

Mirfield Viaduct brought the line to Battyeford where the goods yard was on the right hand side. The station had wooden buildings but brick platforms which extended at the Huddersfield end onto Battyeford Viaduct. This was a brick structure which led directly onto the girder bridge spanning the River Calder.

The Leeds New Line came alongside the Cald Valley route by Heaton Lodge Junction but made r physical contact at that point. Instead it passed und by means of a twin arched bridge and then joined th 'old' Leeds – Huddersfield line at what was initial known as Heckmondwike Junction but rename Spen Valley Junction by the LMS.

A local service was provided between Leeds ar Huddersfield via the 'New Line'. In 1910 there we some 13 trains each way more or less evenly space throughout the day. There was of course no suc thing as a regular interval timetable in those days. A on many routes, there was an extra train each way c a Saturday lunchtime and another in the late evenir at 11 pm from Leeds and 11.10 from Huddersfiel Journey time was about 50 minutes and most trair stopped at all stations. A few missed Farnley Wortley and Bradley which were also served by trair on the Dewsbury route. There was never a booke passenger service on a Sunday when the signal boxe were closed if not required by special traffic.

After a reduction during the First World War th number of trains using the 'New Line' was restore and in 1938 there were 14 Monday to Friday trains plu Saturday extras. Cuts made during the Second Wor War were never fully restored. In 1948 there were on six with an 8¾ hour gap during the day except c Saturdays when there were three extras. Bearing mind the density of population, the train service ha sunk beyond the point where it was worthwhile.

Birstall Town Station closed in July 1951 though casional excursions continued to call. Cleckheaton ɔen followed in January 1953 having allegedly been tronised by only ten people daily. A few months er, BR made known to local authorities their ention to close the remaining stations on the line. pposition to the closures fizzled away and the last in left Huddersfield at 10.33 pm on Saturday October 1953.

The line remained in use for both local and through ight traffic as well as certain passenger trains. It as decided to route some of the diesel services this ay in 1961 because the extra two miles was con- lered to be adequately compensated by the reduced k of signal stops on the Dewsbury route.

The Beeching Report spelt the end. The local goods rds were all closed and in September 1964 through ssenger trains were diverted via Dewsbury apart m the 3 p.m. from Liverpool Lime Street to wcastle. This continued to travel via the Spen lley whilst the farce was enacted of inviting objec- ns to the T.U.C.C. Class 40 No. D395 hauled the al working on Saturday 31 July 1965.

The only outstanding obstacle to complete closure as the oil terminal at Liversedge which had been ened in November 1963 for the delivery of fuel oil. is was the sort of traffic which BR claimed it wished handle. In January 1966, a short spur was opened rough Heckmondwike goods yard so that traffic to versedge Spen could run direct from Healey Mills marshalling yard via the ex L&Y route. The rest of the Leeds New Line was then abandoned. Much of it has been redeveloped. The tracks are still in place between Thornhill, Heckmondwike and Liversedge Spen but there has been no oil traffic since 1986.

The signal box at Gildersome East, typical of those on the Leeds New Line. *(John Holroyd)*

A 'Trans Pennine' unit drops down towards Gildersome Tunnel with the 4.00 pm Liverpool Lime Street – Hull on 3 August 1964. *(M. Mitchell)*

Upper Birstall Station (renamed Birstall Town in 1935) viewed from Gelderd Road shortly after opening. The wooden structure was typical of stations on the 'New Line'.
(G.S. Cooper collection)

'Jubilee' 4-6-0 No. 45581 'Bihar and Orissa' passing Birstall Town with the 11 am from Leeds City on 30 June 1962. The station had been removed following closure in 1951.
(Anne Baughan)

Cleckheaton Spen Station was only accessible from the town by means of a road viaduct provided by the LNWR.
(Anne Baughan)

'Black Five' No. 44780 pauses at Liversedge Spen with a Huddersfield to Leeds local in August 1953. *(Roy Brook)*

Battyeford Station and staff. A view towards Leeds. *(Roy Brook collection)*

A complete six-car Trans Pennine set has just come under the Calder Valley route at Heaton Lodge on 11 March 1961. This short stretch of the 'Leeds New Line' now accommodates the burrowing junction. *(Martin Bairstow collection)*

The Birstall Branch

The two mile branch to Birstall was authorised by the original Leeds, Dewsbury & Manchester Railway Act of 1845. The single track branch opened on 30 September 1852. Proposals to extend the branch to Bradford were rejected in 1861 in favour of the GNR branch from Adwalton Junction to Batley. Birstall was condemned to remain a backwater.

The 1880 timetable shows 12 trains each way, except on Sundays, designed as far as possible to connect at Batley for both Leeds and Huddersfield. The one intermediate station, Carlinghow, had opened in 1872.

In 1875 the Dewsbury, Batley & Birstall Tramway Company commenced a horse tram service between those towns. This was converted to steam operation in 1879, extended to Gomersal in 1881 and fina electrified and extended to Birkenshaw in 1905 whe it met but could not join the non-standard gau Bradford Tramways. With very low speeds, spart passenger accommodation and four different gaug within West Yorkshire, the trams were no threat longer distance railway services and most of the traf they carried was purely local. But the Birstall bran railway was no match to a ten minute interval tra service. By 1910, the number of trains had fallen 4 per day and the passenger service ceased as 'temporary' war time measure at the end of 1916. T branch remained in use for goods traffic until 196 thirty years after the demise of the parallel tramwa

An LNWR 0-6-0 heads three coaches from Birstall towards Carlinghow about the turn of the century.
(G.S. Cooper collection)

WD 2-8-0 No. 90694 has just left Batley with the Birstall branch goods on the morning of 25 May 1962. *(John Holroyd)*

Sister engine No. 90680 approaching the Birstall terminus on 1 June 1962. *(John Holroyd)*

On 16 June 1962, L&Y 0-6-0 No. 52515 was specially cleaned at Sowerby Bridge shed to work the final goods to Birstall. It is seen in Carlinghow Station during a photographic stop on the return trip. *(John Holroyd)*

'he Midland Railway Huddersfield 'Branch'

In 1898 the Midland Railway embarked upon its Vest Riding Lines' which involved a cut off to its nglo Scottish main line between Royston and radford, together with new lines into Dewsbury and uddersfield. The original scheme would have meant third railway in the Spen Valley but this was dropped favour of running powers over stretches of L&Y. ne project was never completed and the commend-ole link across Bradford was abandoned as a result of e First World War. It is a great pity that the branches to Dewsbury and Huddersfield could not have been crificed instead. They achieved little more than to emonstrate that the age of uncontrolled railway pansion was still alive in the first decade of the esent century.

The Dewsbury branch opened to goods in 1906. om a flying junction with the MR Royston – Thorn-hill line at Middlestown it crossed over the Calder Valley main line to finish at Savile Town which was to have become Dewsbury's fourth separate railway terminus. In the event it never saw a passenger train and closed in 1950.

Opened in 1910 the Huddersfield branch was just as grand. A single track but with formation wide enough for double, it left the L&Y at Mirfield Junction and crossed the Colne Valley by a viaduct near Bradley. It came to a separate terminus at Newtown where the Midland hoped to establish its Huddersfield passenger station. Some 64 years earlier the LNW and L&Y had managed to integrate their facilities at Huddersfield. The Midland Railway evidently thought that its customers would prefer to be deposited further away from the town centre and with no connecting services.

There never was a passenger service. In 1923 the LMS opened a junction at Red Doles to give access to Newtown goods depot from the ex LNW main line. This enabled coal wagons to reach Huddersfield gas works without having to go via Mirfield. The gas works was served by a line running down the street from the ex Midland goods yard and under the LNWR viaduct. It was laid by Huddersfield Corporation and opened in 1923. The provision of Red Doles Junctio had the effect of relegating the Mirfield – Red Dole section of the Midland line to wagon storage. It close completely in 1937 though the viaduct at Bradle remains as a monument to this rather foolish projec Newtown yard closed in 1968, the gas works lir having closed two years earlier.

A coal train passing along Fitzwilliam Street in Huddersfield on its way from the gas works to the Midland goods yard at Newtown during 1960. *(P. Sunderland)*

The Kirkburton Branch

When the LNWR announced plans to build a branch to Kirkburton, there was local pressure to try and persuade the company to continue a further 5 miles to the mining village of Clayton West. The LNWR considered that the potential traffic did not justify the cost of constructing what would have been a difficult line.

On learning in 1862 that the Midland Railway was interested in a route from Barnsley to Huddersfield through Clayton West and Kirkburton, the LNWR resolved to press ahead with its branch as far as Kirkburton and succeeded in gaining Parliamentary sanction on 28 July 1863.

In April 1865 the LNWR reached agreement that if the Midland Railway were to construct a line between Barnsley and Kirkburton, the LNWR would abandon its proposed terminus there and contribute the money saved towards a joint station with the Midland. The LNWR would grant the Midland running powers into Huddersfield in return for reciprocal powers to Barnsley. The Midland scheme did not go ahead. In time the Lancashire & Yorkshire Railway provided a branch to the village of Clayton West but it was not until 1983 that a direct train service commenced between Huddersfield and Barnsley.

The LNWR went ahead with the Kirkburton branch as a single line, though with an optimism which characterised such projects, they took enough land

An LNWR 2-4-2T restarts a Kirkburton to Huddersfield trair of six-wheel compartment coaches from the stop at Kirkheaton.
(David Joy collectior

›r double track. Completion of the line was set back ›hen on 15 February 1866 one of the seven arches ›mprising Whitacre Mill viaduct fell into the canal. ›his viaduct was situated just beyond the junction at ›eighton where the branch turned more than 90 ›egrees to head south east towards Kirkburton. The ›ilway ran through the bottom of the valley but ›nfortunately the intermediate population lived higher ›p the hillside. At Kirkburton there was a height ›ifference of some 400 yards and distance of half a ›ile between village and station.

At the opening of the branch on Monday 7 October ›367, Mr Duffield, deputy locomotive superintendent ›f the LNWR referred to the possibility of going on to ›arnsley and of doubling the track. He advised the ›ilway's new Kirkburton customers that 'if they ›quired any alterations in any of the present ›rrangements they had only to be made known to the ›irectors and, if they considered it would be wise to ›ake them, he had no doubt they would at once agree ›› them.'

According to the *Huddersfield Examiner* 'Kirkheaton › a pretty little station and at it full arrangements have ›een made for the carrying on of the goods and ›assenger traffic of the district.' This announcement ›as a little premature in that goods traffic could not be ›andled immediately as the warehouses were ›complete. However, arrangements were made for ›eight traffic to start at the beginning of 1868.

The 1880 timetable is set out below:

LNWR HUDDERSFIELD - KIRKBURTON NOV 1880

	am	am	am	SX pm	SO pm	pm	pm	pm	pm	pm	SO pm
HUDDERSFIELD	6 55	8 05	10 15	12 40	1 05	2 30	4 47	5 50	6 55	8 13	10 20
DEIGHTON	7 01	8 11	10 21	12 46	1 11	2 39	4 53	5 56	7 01	8 19	10 26
KIRKHEATON	7 04	8 14	10 24	12 49	1 14	2 43	4 57	6 00	7 04	8 23	10 29
FENAY BRIDGE	7 08	8 18	10 28	12 53	1 18	2 47	5 01	6 04	7 08	8 27	10 33
KIRKBURTON	7 13	8 23	10 33	12 58	1 23	2 52	5 05	6 08	7 12	8 32	10 38

	am	am	am	pm	pm	pm	pm	SO pm	pm	SO pm	
KIRKBURTON	7 20	8 30	10 40	2 00	3 00	5 15	6 15	7 20	8 45	10 55	
FENAY BRIDGE	7 24	8 34	10 44	2 04	3 05	5 19	6 19	7 25	8 50	11 00	
KIRKHEATON	7 28	8 38	10 48	2 08	3 09	5 23	6 23	7 29	8 54	11 04	
DEIGHTON	7 31	8 42	10 51	2 11	3 12	5 27	6 28	7 32	8 58	11 08	
HUDDERSFIELD	7 40	8 50	11 00	2 20	3 21	5 35	6 38	7 40	9 05	11 15	

NO SUNDAY SERVICE ALL TRAINS 1, 2 AND 3 CLASS
SX - SATURDAYS EXCEPTED SO - SATURDAYS ONLY

The 1910 timetable shows a slight improvement over the intervening 30 years with 3 additional trains including a 5.45 a.m. from Kirkburton which must have worked out their empty stock. The branch was never favoured with a Sunday service and fell an early victim to bus competition. In 1930 the LMS conceded that the indirect route and remoteness of the branch stations made perseverance with passenger trains futile and withdrew them in favour of participation in the Huddersfield Joint Omnibus Committee.

The pick-up goods made its way up to Kirkburton until 1965. A siding at Deighton perpetuated the first few yards of the branch until 1971.

Ex LNWR 0-8-0 No. 49323 passing through the remains of Deighton Station with the Kirkburton goods on 6 August 1960. *(Neil Fraser)*

An LNWR 2-4-2T calls at Kirkheaton en route for Kirkburton.
(Roy Brook collection)

Standard 2-6-4T No. 80044 at Kirkburton with a rail tour on 2 May 1959. *(J.C.W. Halliday)*

Coal traffic was still being received at Kirkburton in August 1961, more than thirty years after the passenger closure.
(Peter E. Baughan)

'he Delph and Oldham Branches

Signalman W. Hobson hands the single line token for the Delph branch to the driver of Fowler 2-6-2T No. 40060 at Delph Junction. *(J. Davenport)*

'he 'Delph Donkey' was a term of endearment for the 'anch train. There is little evidence that horse power 'as actually used in the early years although the pos-bility was referred to in the Government Inspector's port authorising opening of the railway to Delph. team power was certainly employed on 1 September 351, opening day of the 1½ mile branch. If a horse as used on the passenger service, it must have been ery briefly until the LNWR found that it was imprac-cal, particularly with the branch train having to averse the main line to Greenfield.

Delph Junction signal box stood half a mile north of reenfield. The single track then ran alongside the ain line for ¼ mile before striking off sharply to the ft. It then twisted with the Tame Valley before aching the single platform terminus alongside Bailey ill.

5 July 1856 saw the opening of the LNWR Green-eld to Oldham line. This climbed at 1 in 100 through ydgate Tunnel to Grotton then descended towards dham. Initially this branch terminated at a station djacent to the L&Y at Oldham Mumps. LNWR ser-ces were extended to Oldham Clegg Street on 1 July 362. The LNWR station at Mumps then closed as oon as Glodwick Road was ready for opening on November 1862. A bay platform was provided at reenfield for Oldham trains terminating there but a oportion of them ran through to Delph.

The 1880 timetable shows six weekday trains to and om Delph but Oldham enjoyed a more frequent ser-ce with connections off most Leeds – Manchester ains including Sundays. By 1910 there were 20 reenfield with 11 going on to Delph. There were just workings on a Sunday only as far as Greenfield.

A much improved service began on 1 January 1912 with the introduction of push-pull working and the opening of additional halts at Grasscroft, Moorgate and Dobcross. Moorgate was situated on the main line just south of Delph Junction. Only Delph trains stopped there. A further halt, named after a nearby mill, opened at Measurements in 1932. It was served by one or two rush hour trains.

The 1938 timetable shows 38 Monday to Friday departures from Clegg St. with 20 continuing to Delph. The first trains are at 5.45 a.m. to Greenfield and 6.25 to Delph. The last services are at 11.00 p.m. to Delph and 11.20 to Greenfield. The Saturday service is of similar standard but with the last Oldham – Delph train put back to 11.27 with an arrival at Delph one minute before midnight. A few trains omit Grasscroft stops. There are 17 Oldham – Greenfield workings on the Sunday timetable.

Ten years later the train service frequency had reduced to about two-thirds of its pre-war standard. This still left it vastly superior to many branch and secondary lines of that period. In the summer of 1953, a Sunday service ran to Delph for the first time. It was repeated in 1954 giving nine departures between 12.15 and 10.30 p.m. However this was not to last and the passenger service was closed between Oldham and Delph at the end of April 1955. A donkey was turned out to pose for photographs and to greet the arrival of 2-6-2T No. 41281 on the 11.10 p.m. from Oldham Clegg Street.

Freight was handled at Delph until November 1963. Most of the branch is now a footpath. The last Oldham – Greenfield goods train operated on 10 April 1964.

With steam heating in full operation, the 4.44 pm to Oldham Clegg Street awaits departure from Delph on 18 April 1955. *(John Oxley)*

Ivatt 2-6-2T No. 41280 passing the rather spartan Measurements Halt bound for Delph on 18 April 1955. *(John Oxley)*

Commuters prepare to board the 5.33 pm push-pull for Oldham at Dobcross. *(John Oxley)*

Moorgate Halt was situated immediately south of Delph Junction but served only by branch trains. 40012 pauses with a push-pull bound for Oldham Clegg Street. *(J. Davenport)*

Standard 2MT 2-6-2T No. 84010 calls at Grasscroft with a Delph to Oldham push-pull. Lydgate Tunnel lies immediately beyond. *(J. Davenport)*

3MT 2-6-2T No. 40059 emerges from Lydgate Tunnel with a Delph push-pull. *(J. Davenport)*

40014 in Lees Station with an Oldham to Delph local. The driving trailer is one of six built by the LNWR in 1911. The intermediate coach is a former LNWR open composite later relegated to third class only with deep set entrance doors. *(J. Davenport)*

Ex LNWR 7F 0-8-0 No. 49428 assisting Ivatt 2MT 2-6-2T No. 41281 on the 8.55 am freight from Oldham Glodwick Road to Delph as it approaches Lees. *(J. Davenport)*

A small group of passengers await the Delph train at Oldham Glodwick Road Station on the last day of service, 30 April 1955. The view is towards Greenfield. *(G.C. Lewthwaite)*

Standard 2-6-2T No. 84012 has just propelled its train from Delph into Oldham Clegg Street on 2 April 1955. *(J.C.W. Halliday)*

The entrance to Clegg Street Station. Passengers changing for L&Y destinations such as Rochdale had merely to cross the road to reach Central Station, just visible on the left. *(J.C.W. Halliday)*

The Oldham Ashton & Guide Bridge Junction Railway

Great Central class C13 4-4-2T No. 67421 has arrived at Oldham Clegg Street from Guide Bridge with a train of clerestory stock. The platform on the right belongs to Central Station but is only accessible via the street. *(P. Hutchinson)*

n 1846 the only railway serving Oldham was the ranch of the Manchester & Leeds which reached Werneth by the 1 in 27 incline. The line was about to e extended to Mumps. The Oldham District Railways, backed by the Manchester & Leeds, proposed a network radiating to Ashton, Saddleworth, Royton nd Rochdale. They were opposed by the Oldham, Manchester, Liverpool & Birkenhead Junction Railway, which despite its title was basically interested in he same thing as the Oldham District. The Oldham, Manchester, Liverpool & Birkenhead Junction Bill won the approval of the House of Commons but was defeated in the Lords. Its promoters then made peace or the 1847 session under the title of the Oldham Alliance Railway. Thoughts of getting to Saddleworth were dropped to avoid opposition from the LNWR who were authorised to build their line from Greenfield to Oldham. The remainder of the Oldham Alliance scheme was authorised but for want of inance was never built – at least not at that stage. All he lines were revived later.

The Manchester, Sheffield & Lincolnshire Railway had itself tried to promote a link from Guide Bridge to Oldham but this had been rejected in favour of the Oldham Alliance. On 18 July 1856, the MS & L eceived a deputation including the Mayors of Oldham and Ashton who prevailed upon the MS & L to build a branch line to Oldham. The railway was sympathetic o the idea but expressed a preference for any scheme to go ahead with the support of the L&Y and LNW Railways. The MS & L evidently did not want a major Parliamentary fight to get into Oldham.

The Oldham, Ashton & Guide Bridge Junction Railway was incorporated on 10 August 1857 with a capital of £150,000. The L&Y had expressed interest in joining the venture but then withdrew leaving the MS & L and LNW companies to subscribe £50,000 each, the rest to be found locally. On 30 June 1862 the line was leased jointly to the MS & L and LNW.

The railway was opened with due ceremony on 31 July 1861, regular services beginning on 26 August. Commencing at a double junction with the MS & L main line west of Guide Bridge the line proceeded through a short-lived station at Ashton Moss to join the L&Y Miles Platting – Stalybridge line at OA & GB Junction. It traversed the L&Y for a few yards then branched off again straight into Ashton Oldham Road Station which was on a sharp curve. A 12 arch viaduct, 200 feet in length carried the line over the Medlock into Park Bridge station.

Oldham Clegg Street had a main platform with a bay at the Guide Bridge end and an island platform. The Lancashire & Yorkshire Railway built its own Central Station adjacent to Clegg Street but linked to it only via the street above. North of Clegg Street there was a junction with the L&Y enabling OA & GB trains to reach Oldham Mumps if they wished. The OA & GB itself continud parallel to the L&Y to make an end-on junction with the LNWR branch from Greenfield to the east of Mumps just before the LNW's Glodwick Road Station.

The MS & LR provided a local service from Guide Bridge to Oldham Glodwick Road. Initially there was an express service from Manchester London Road to Oldham Glodwick Road. These trains completed the journey in 25 minutes with stops only at Ardwick, Ashton Oldham Road and Oldham Clegg Street. In 1876 the LNWR opened a link from Crowthorne Junction on the OA & GB, half a mile north of Guide Bridge, to Denton Junction and was able to introduce an Oldham to Stockport service from 1 April.

The 1910 timetable shows 24 weekday trains between Guide Bridge and Oldham Glodwick Road with 11 on Sundays. The LNWR offered 10 trains each weekday from Stockport to Oldham Clegg Street where 4 of them terminated. Three of the others continued to Glodwick Road, one went non-stop to Huddersfield and the other 2 crossed onto the L&Y to reach Mumps then Rochdale. One of these conveyed through carriages from Euston to Rochdale – a facility which that town lacks nowadays. There were just two Stockport – Oldham trains on Sundays.

'Bradshaw' for 1957 manages to consolidate both the former LNER and LMSR services over the OA & GB. There was now no Sunday service and, except on Saturdays, a huge gap during the day time with no departure from Clegg Street between 9.16 and 4.22.

Clegg Street was the northern limit of operatio[n] Glodwick Road having closed in 1955. Connections t[o] Rochdale are shown together with a warning tha[t] 'passengers must change from Clegg Street t[o] Central Station or vice-versa at Oldham'. There is n[o] mention of the fact that they were adjacent.

Some longer distance passengers from Oldham Ashton and even Rochdale may have found the OA & GB convenient for avoiding the gap across Manchester. Ashton passengers could have done this just as well from Park Parade station if that had not been closed for no apparent reason in 1956.

As regards local traffic, the OA & GB service of trains to Stockport and 6 to Guide Bridge, augmented slightly on Saturdays had probably sunk to the point where it was irrelevant. BR decided in 1958 that the standard of service required by Oldham was a dmu every 20 minutes to Manchester Victoria via the L&Y Hollinwood line. This still operates albeit now half hourly.

The OA & GB passenger service was withdrawn in May 1959 but the line remained in use for freight and for the parcels depot at Clegg Street. Major repair work was carried out on Park Bridge viaduct during 1960 but this was dismantled early in 1971 following complete closure in 1967 of the line between OA & GB Junction and Clegg Street. The parcels depot there remained, served from the L&Y line, until BR abandoned this class of traffic in 1981.

Sporting the 26F code for Lees Shed, Aspinall 3F 0-6-0 No. 52410 (built 1900 withdrawn 1960) nears Oldham Clegg Street with a local from Stockport. *(J. Davenport)*

The volume of parcels handled at Clegg Street required a fleet of road vehicles.
(J.C.W. Halliday)

C13 4-4-2T No. 67417 between Park Bridge and Oldham with a train from Guide Bridge.
(J. Davenport)

Ex WD 2-8-0 No. 90140 crossing Park Bridge Viaduct with a freight from Ashton Moss to Oldham Glodwick Road.
(J. Davenport)

Fairburn class 4MT 2-6-4T No. 42114 at Park Bridge with the 4.31 pm Huddersfield to Stockport.
(J. Davenport)

An Oldham Clegg Street to Guide Bridge 'motor train' is propelled into Oldham Road Station at Ashton by class C13 4-4-2T No. 67421.
(J. Davenport)

The 11.18 Oldham Clegg Street to Stockport calls at Ashton Oldham Road on 2 May 1959 hauled by Ivatt 2MT 2-6-2T No. 41206. *(P. Hutchinson)*

A train of clerestory stock hauled by No. 67417 negotiates OA & GB Junction on 30 August 1958. The train has come off the Guide Bridge line on the left behind the signal box and is about to enter Ashton Oldham Road Station. The overbridge was later demolished and the box replaced by one of BR pattern at track level. *(P. Hutchinson)*

Lees Shed in the 1950s

by Jim Davenport

Lees Shed opened in 1878 to replace an earlier depot in Oldham. It closed along with the Oldham to Greenfield line on 10 April 1964. An array of LMS tank engines stand outside the shed on 4 April 1954. *(P. Hutchinson)*

The ex LNWR Motive Power Depot at Lees was situated on the north side of the Oldham to Greenfield line just east of Lees Station. It had an allocation of about twenty locomotives and employed about 40 drivers and 40 firemen. Most of the work was out and home. Very little relieving work was done.

During my period as Depot Clerk from 1952 until 1960, the duties were varied and covered any clerical work involved in the functioning of the Shed. My job included the calculation of time worked and payment of staff, general personnel matters, stores, statistics and costings both for engines and for men. I also had to post late notices of engineering work etc.

On the London Midland Region, a lot of work was carried out at individual depots which I believe was done at headquarters on Eastern and North Eastern Regions such as calculation of time and a lot of statistics.

In the early 1950s, the only Class 4 mixed traffic 2-6-4T allocated was No. 42551. It worked the following diagram:

06.15	Stalybridge – Stockport	Passenger
07.55	Stockport – Manchester	Passenger
09.35	Manchester Victoria – Oldham Mumps	Passenger
16.52	Oldham Clegg Street – Leeds	Passenger
(18.20) (ex Hull)	Leeds – Manchester Exchange	Fish

On Saturdays

06.15	Stalybridge – Stockport	Passenge
07.55	Stockport – Manchester Victoria	Passenge
10.45	Manchester Victoria – Rochdale	Passenge
12.15	Rochdale – Oldham Mumps	Passenge

Further Class 4MTs were brought to Lees to cope wit an increase in parcels following the opening of th parcels concentration depot at Oldham Clegg Stree from which trains were worked by Lees engines t Stockport, Manchester Victoria, Wakefield an Crewe. A 4MT used to run light engine from Lees vi the 1 in 27 Werneth Incline to Middleton whence worked a passenger train to Manchester Victori before taking up parcels workings.

The smaller Fowler Class 3MT 2-6-2 tanks came i two varieties. Lees had six with vacuum control fc push-pull workings and two without this facility. On of the non vacuum control fitted engines worked th following diagram:

06.45	Stalybridge – Leeds	Passenge
	Leeds – Huddersfield	ECS
16.21	Huddersfield – Stockport	Passenge
19.05	Stockport – Oldham Clegg Street	Passenge

On Saturdays

12.27	Greenfield – Stockport	Passenge
14.28	Stockport – Manchester Victoria	Passenge
16.25	Manchester Victoria – Royton	Passenge

The 14.28 from Stockport was the only Class 1 xpress passenger) train regularly worked by Lees. ne other non fitted loco was used as spare to cover e Class 4MT for wash out etc.

The push-pull fitted locos worked the ldham – Delph, Stalybridge – Stockport and ldham – Stockport services and also the Delph anch goods. The Fowler 2-6-2Ts were tricky ngines to fire and were heavy on maintenance articularly springs. When they were replaced by Ivatt nd BR Class 2MT 2-6-2 tanks in 1954, nobody was ally sorry to see them go.

The ex L&Y 0-6-0s generally worked shunting and ip duties in the Oldham area. A sample diagram ould be:

.50 Oldham Glodwick Road – Diggle empties
Shunt at Diggle
.00 Diggle – Oldham Glodwick Road
Light engine to Lees
Light engine to Glodwick Road – shunt
.10 Oldham Glodwick Road to Ashton Oldham Road
Shunt at Ashton Oldham Road
Light engine to Lees Shed

On occasions they worked passenger deputising for ne Fowler 3MT tanks but never on the Delph branch. the early fifties, they had a diagramed passenger urn working the 07.40 Greenfield to Stockport then nto Edgeley Shed whence it did a trip working to lacclesfield. The following day it returned to Lees via ne 18.52 Heaton Norris – Diggle goods. This diagram alternated with a 4F from Stockport.

On one occasion an L&Y 0-6-0 worked a passenger service to Leeds, tender first and without loss of time deputising for a 2-6-4T which had derailed coming off the shed. During Oldham Wakes holiday there was a relief from Clegg Street to Skegness rostered as far as Guide Bridge for an 0-6-0, usually No. 52248, with nine or ten coaches which had been stabled in Lees goods yard. In the early 1960s the veteran L&Y 0-6-0s were replaced by Ivatt 2-6-0 locomotives.

In the early fifties, heavier freights were in the hands of Fowler 7F 0-8-0s. They worked from Oldham Glodwick Road, Greenfield, Diggle and Staley & Millbrook to Healey Mills and Wakefield. They worked to Stockport and round the Oldham loop including the 1 in 27 Werneth Incline and from Ashton Moss to Brindle Heath. Despite not being vacuum fitted, they were rostered on the 17.40 Lees to Stockport which was class F. This was one of the reasons for their replacement by austerity Class 8F locos.

In later years Lees had no turntable but the engine diagrams were usually arranged so that they came back to the shed facing the right way. Normally the tank engines faced chimney first towards Yorkshire.

Lees drivers and firemen worked mostly on their own engines but they had some turns on locos from other sheds. They were booked to work a Longsight 8F, which in practice could be anything from a Midland 3F upwards even a 2-6-4T on one occasion. This worked the 05.20 Stockport to Oldham freight then the 11.20 Guide Bridge – Millbrook and 13.31

Ex L&Y class 3F 0-6-0 No. 52410 shunting at Diggle. *(J. Davenport)*

Millbrook – Healey Mills. It stabled at Mirfield and then worked a freight to Diggle and the 10.22 Diggle to Mold Junction freight the following morning.

Lees men also worked between Stockport and Diggle on a Huddersfield Class 5 and between Diggle and Stalybridge with a Mirfield engine which alternated with a Lees 7F or 8F.

Special passenger work took Lees men on workings from the Diggle – Stalybridge area to Blackpool, Southport, Morecambe, Llandudno, Shrewsbury, Leeds and York. Often this was on borrowed engines but Lees 2-6-4 tanks had apparatus for picking up on water troughs and could work through to Blackpool and Southport.

With the opening of Clegg Street parcels concentration depot, there were special workings at times of peak mail order demand such as Christmas and when a new catalogue was out. Lees men worked specials to Carlisle, Wigan, Willesden Junction, Crewe, Shrewsbury, Wakefield and York. Again moti power was generally borrowed but the 2-6-4 tanks d work to Crewe.

Lees men were the first in the area to work a 350 h diesel shunter on engineering trains in Standedg tunnel in the late 1940s. This happened again in th 1950s when engines were 'imported' from Hu Springhead Shed because the tunnel was then in th North Eastern Region. In the early 1960s 204 h diesel mechanical shunters built by Yorkshire Engin Co were employed at Clegg Street parcels depot bu they were neither heavy nor powerful enough an were replaced by 350 hp locos of what is now Class 08

There was no regular Sunday work at Lees She except during the brief period when the Delph branc had a Summer service. There was however wo most Sundays on ballast and engineering trains and i Summer on excursion trains from the Saddlewort area.

Fowler 7F 0-8-0 No. 49618 outside Lees shed.
(J. Davenport)

Standard 2-6-2 tanks came to Lees shed in 1954. No. 84019 was push-pull fitted.
(J. Davenport)

onclusion

the story of the Standedge Line, the lowest ebb ust have been reached about 1968. What sort of anagement could possibly have believed that it uld head off motorway competition simply by moving Huddersfield stops from certain trains hich still remained slower than some with calls at th Huddersfield and Stalybridge. If that kind of ilosophy has prevailed then it is not impossible to agine the Standedge Line going the same way as oodhead.

Against that background, the achievements of cent years become all the more remarkable. When e first edition of this book was published in 1984, the el of passenger service was at least as good as it d ever been previously. Now the frequency is three nes what it was only a few years ago.

When the size of the BR passenger network was abilized in the 1970s after the mass closures of the s, it was on the basis that both the levels of service d of subsidy would be more or less frozen. The late 80s have seen an increase in service linked to a duction in subsidy. This situation has been largely derwritten by improvements in productivity and by reliability of the new rolling stock. Something has d to give and the most noticeable effect on travels is the severe overcrowding which arises not just at normal peak travel times but at the artificial ones eated by the fares policy being pursued by the West rkshire PTE.

Many Standedge Line expresses are only two car mations but they do seat far more passengers per ach than their predecessors thanks to their length d to the removal of first class accommodation and n space. They are being rostered for traffic all year und to the limit of their availability which is much her than that of earlier motive power and rolling ck. There is hardly any spare capacity to cover for ergencies and virtually nothing for seasonal imbalces in the flow of traffic. At peak holiday times, ny passengers are carried in appalling conditions. BR claim that they are the victims of their own ccess. The test is whether they will build on that ccess. There is certainly no shortage of ideas for the development of services but resources are stretched to the limit. We are promised that the risk of cancelled and/or shortened trains will remain high until the 158s are fully operational. After this there are no plans to build any further diesel trains. Already there are signs that reliability of the over worked 150s is falling and no doubt the 156s will follow.

The past few years have witnessed tremendous progress but with cost saving always a prime consideration. If carried too far this is false economy.

So much for the main line but what of the branches which were so cheerfully discarded a quarter of a century ago? It was claimed that only one commuter boarded the 8.00 a.m. to Leeds at Birstall Town immediately prior to closure in 1951 and that less than ten people a day used Cleckheaton Spen. One can only speculate how many would now be cancelling their saverstrips or brandishing their metro cards. There are now far more people travelling to city centre office jobs and shopping habits have also changed. Traffic congestion and parking problems had barely surfaced in the early 1950s. Journey times by bus were credible in those days. Today the Leeds New Line would do good business in the Spen Valley and at Gomersal and Birstall.

The line between Greenfield and Oldham might also be busy now if it had survived. It was always treated as a branch and operated in close association with the Delph Donkey. Long distance rail traffic from Oldham today must be negligible. Perhaps the North Wales train should be running not through Stalybridge but from Greenfield to Manchester Victoria via Oldham Mumps. Maybe it should run through from Scarborough. If the route were still available, these possibilities would surely be considered. Unfortunately the policy in the 1960s was not merely to close railways but to destroy their rights of way and that is a process which still continues on abandoned lines. How ironic that the Delph branch and the Micklehurst Loop are largely conserved as footpaths yet the lines which could potentially find renewed railway use have been sold off piecemeal for redevelopment. That is a familiar story.

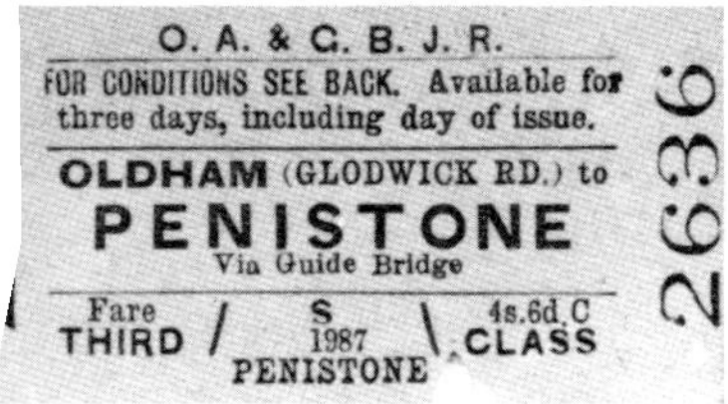

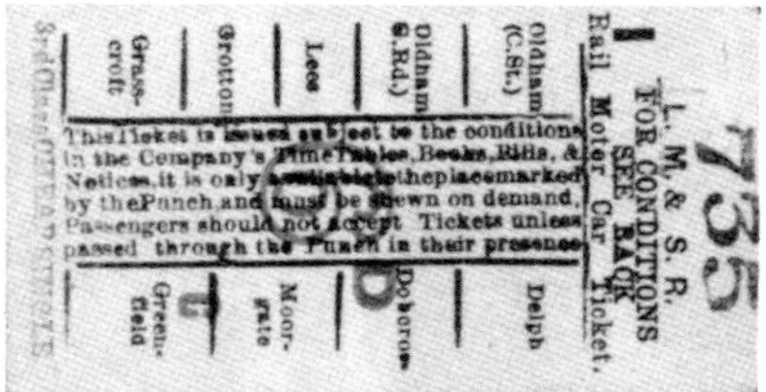

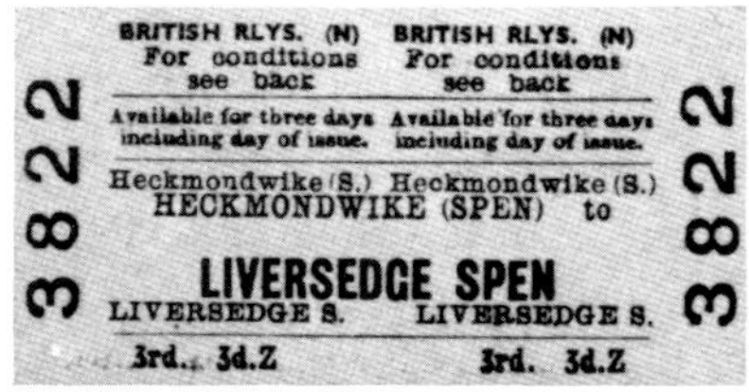

Tickets from the collection of G.C. Lewthwaite including a Delph 'railmotor' ticket.

Appendices

Opening of lines

7. 7.1840	Ardwick Jct – Manchester
5.10.1840	Thornhill LNW Jct – Heaton Lodge Jct (L&Y)
17.11.1841	Guide Bridge – Ardwick Jct (MS&L)
1. 1.1844	Miles Platting – Manchester Victoria (L&Y)
23.12.1845	Stalybridge – Guide Bridge (MS&L)
13. 4.1846	Ashton Charlestown – Miles Platting (L&Y)
30. 6.1846	Leeds Wellington – Whitehall Junction (Mid)
5.10.1846	Stalybridge – Ashton Charlestown (L&Y)
2. 8.1847	Heaton Lodge Junction – Huddersfield
18. 9.1848	Leeds Central – Thornhill LNW Jct
1. 8.1849	Huddersfield – Stalybridge
1.10.1850	Whitehall Juction – Coply Hill Junction
1. 9.1851	Greenfield (Delph Jct) – Delph
30. 9.1852	Batley – Birstall
5. 7.1856	Greenfield – Oldham
26. 8.1861	Oldham – Guide Bridge (OA&GB)
2. 4.1866	Farnley Jct – Farnley Siding (goods)
7.10.1867	Deighton – Kirkburton
1. 3.1882	Canal Jct – Farnley Jct
1.12.1885	Diggle – Micklehurst – Stalybridge (goods)
3. 5.1886	Diggle – Micklehurst – Stalybridge (passenger)
18. 9.1899	Northorpe – Spen Valley Jct (goods)
9. 7.1900	Farnley Jct – Northorpe (goods)
1.10.1900	Farnley Jct – Spen Valley Jct (passenger)
1.11.1910	Mirfield Jct – Huddersfield Newtown (goods) (Mid)
18.12.1911	Ashton Moss – Ashton Moss North Jct (GC)

Closure of lines to passenger traffic

31.12.1916	Diggle – Friezland – Stalybridge (local)
31.12.1916	Batley – Birstall
28. 7.1930	Huddersfield – Kirkburton
3.10.1953	Leeds – Heckmondwike – Huddersfield (local)
30. 4.1955	Oldham Clegg Street – Greenfield – Delph
2. 5.1959	Oldham Clegg Street – Guide Bridge

Closure of lines to all traffic

10. 8.1937	Mirfield Jct – Red Doles Jct
June 1938	Guide Bridge N. Jct – Guide Bridge W. Jct
16. 6.1962	Batley – Birstall
2.11.1963	Greenfield (Delph Jct) – Delph
10. 4.1964	Greenfield – Oldham
3. 4.1965	Deighton – Kirkburton
27.11.1965	Heckmondwike – Spen Valley Junction
9. 1.1966	Farnley Junction – Liversedge
29.10.1966	Diggle – Staley & Millbrook
20. 5.1967	Oldham Clegg St – OA&GB Junction
3. 8.1968	Red Doles Jct – Huddersfield Newtown
30. 1.1971	Kirkburton Junction – Deighton
1972	Staley & Millbrook – Stalybridge

Temporary Closures

Gildersome	1. 8.1917 – 5. 5.1919
Churwell	1. 1.1917 – 1. 3.1920
Staincliffe & Batley Carr	1. 1.1917 – 5. 5.1919
Grasscroft	16. 1.1917 – 1. 1.1919

Stations reopened

Deighton	26. 4.1982
Slaithwaite	12.12.1982
Churwell (as Cottingley)	25. 4.1988

Passenger Stations

Miles			Station	Opened	Closed
0	0		Leeds City	30. 6.1846	–
			Leeds Central	18. 9.1848	29. 4.19
2	2		Farnley & Wortley	8.10.1848	1.11.19
	3¾		Gildersome	1.10.1900	9. 7.19
	6¾		Upper Birstall	1.10.1900	31. 7.19
	8		Gomersal	1.10.1900	3.10.19
	9½		Cleckheaton Spen	1.10.1900	3. 1.19
	10½		Liversedge Spen	1.10.1900	3.10.19
	11¼		Heckmondwike Spen	1.10.1900	3.10.19
	13		Northorpe Higher	1.10.1900	3.10.19
	14¼		Battyeford	1.10.1900	3.10.19
3¼			Churwell	18. 9.1848	30.11.19
4¾			Morley Low	18. 9.1848	–
		0	Birstall	30. 9.1852	31.12.19
		1	Carlinghow	1. 4.1872	31.12.19
8		2	Batley	18. 9.1848	–
8½			Staincliffe & Batley Carr	1.11.1878	5. 4.19
9¼			Dewsbury Wellington Road	18. 9.1848	–
10¾			Ravensthorpe & Thornhill	1. 9.1891	–
12¼			Mirfield	Apr 1845	–
13¼			Heaton Lodge	3. 8.1847	31.10.18
14½	16		Bradley	3. 8.1847	4. 3.19
		0	Kirkburton	7.10.1867	28. 7.19
		1½	Fenay Bridge & Lepton	7.10.1867	28. 7.19
		2¾	Kirkheaton	7.10.1867	28. 7.19
15¼	16¾	4¼	Deighton	30. 8.1871	28. 7.19
17¼	18¾	6¼	Huddersfield	3. 8.1847	–
19	20½		Longwood & Milnsbridge	1. 8.1849	5.10.19
20¼	21¾		Golcar	1. 8.1849	5.10.19
21¾	23¼		Slaithwaite	1. 8.1849	5.10.19
24¼	25¾		Marsden	1. 8.1849	–
28	29½		Diggle	1. 8.1849	5.10.19
	30¾		Uppermill	3. 5.1886	31.12.19
	32		Friezland	3. 5.1886	31.12.19
	34		Micklehurst	3. 5.1886	30. 4.19
	35¼		Staley & Millbrook	3. 5.1886	31.10.19
29¼			Saddleworth	1. 8.1849	5.10.19
		0	Delph	1. 9.1851	30. 4.19
		½	Measurements	18., 7.1932	30. 4.19
		1	Dobcross	1. 1.1912	30. 4.19
29¾		1¾	Moorgate	1. 1.1912	30. 4.19
30¼		2¼	Greenfield	1. 8.1849	–
32½			Mossley	1. 8.1849	–
35	36½		Stalybridge	23.12.1845	–
	37¾		Ashton Park Parade	23.12.1845	3.11.19
	38¼		Dukinfield Central	23.12.1845	2. 5.19
36½			Ashton Charlestown	13. 4.1846	–
		2¾	Grasscroft	1. 1.1912	30. 4.1
		4	Grotton & Springhead	5. 7.1856	30. 4.1
		4¾	Lees	5. 7.1856	30. 4.1
		6	Oldham Glodwick Road	1.11.1862	30. 4.1
		6¼	Oldham Mumps (LNWR)	5. 7.1856	31.10.1
		6½	Oldham Clegg Street	26. 8.1861	2. 5.1
		8¼	Park Bridge	26. 8.1861	2. 5.1
		10	Ashton Oldham Road	26. 8.1861	2. 5.1
		10¾	Ashton Moss	26. 8.1861	Feb 1
	39	11¾	Guide Bridge	17.11.1841	–
	40¼		Fairfield	17.11.1841	–
	41¼		Gorton & Openshaw	23. 5.1842	–
	42¼		Ashburys	July 1855	–
	43		Ardwick	Nov 1842	–
	43¾		Manchester Piccadilly	8. 5.1842	–
38¼			Droylsden	13. 4.1846	5.10.1
39¾			Clayton Bridge	13. 4.1846	5.10.1
40¾			Park	13. 4.1846	–
41½			Miles Platting	1. 1.1844	–
43			Manchester Victoria	1. 1.1844	–
43¼			Manchester Exchange	30. 6.1884	4. 5.1